Oxford
International
Primary

2

Computing
Student Book

Alison Page

Diane Levine

OXFORD

Contents

Introduction

Delivering computing to young learners

Oxford International Primary and Lower Secondary Computing is a complete syllabus for computing education for ages 5–14 (Years 1–9). By following the program of learning set out in this series, teachers can feel reassured that their students have access to the computing skills and understanding that they need for their future education.

Find out more at:
www.oxfordprimary.com/computing.

Structure of the book

This book is divided into six chapters, for Year 2 (ages 6–7).

1 **The nature of technology:** Introduction to the different parts of a computer

2 **Digital literacy:** Finding information on the internet

3 **Computational thinking:** Planning how to solve a problem

4 **Programming:** Making a program with a simple loop

5 **Multimedia:** Making a document with a computer

6 **Numbers and data:** Using a spreadsheet to do sums

What you will find in each unit

- Introduction: An offline activity and a class discussion help students to start thinking about the topic.
- Lessons: Six lessons guide students through activity-based learning.
- Check what you know: A test and activities allow you to measure students' progress.

What you will find in the lessons

Although each lesson is unique, they have common features: learning outcomes for each lesson are set out at the start; learning content delivers skills and develops understanding.

Activity Every lesson involves a learning activity for the students.

Extra challenge Activities to extend students who are able to do more.

Think again Questions check students' understanding of the lesson.

Additional features

You will also find these features throughout the book:

Word cloud The word cloud builds vocabulary by identifying key terms from the unit.

Be creative Suggestions for creative and artistic work.

Explore more Extra tasks that can be taken outside the classroom and into the home.

Digital citizen of the future Advice on using computers responsibly in life.

Glossary Key terms are identified in the text and defined in the glossary at the end.

Assessing student achievement

The final pages in each unit give an opportunity to assess student achievement.

- Developing: This acknowledges the achievement of students who find the content challenging but have made progress.
- Secure: Students have reached the level set out in the programme for their age group. Most should reach this level.
- Extended: This recognises the achievement of students who have developed above-average skills and understanding.

Questions and activities are colour-coded according to achievement level. Self-evaluation advice helps students to check their own progress.

Software to use

We recommend Scratch for writing programs at this age. For other lessons, teachers can use any suitable software, for example: Microsoft Office; Google Drive software; LibreOffice; any web browser.

Source files

 You will see this symbol on some of the pages.

This means that there are extra files you can access to help with the learning activities. For example, Scratch programming files and downloadable images.

To access the files, go to **www.oxfordowl.co.uk** and navigate to the 'Oxford International Primary Programme' page then 'Oxford International Primary Computing'.

Teacher's Guides

For more on these topics, look at the Teacher's Guide that accompanies this book.

The nature of technology: Our computers

You will learn

- → what are the main parts of a computer
- → what the main parts of a computer are for
- → things computers can and cannot do.

Computers are all around us.

Computers are in our phones. Computers are in our homes.

Computers can help us learn and do our work.

You need to learn to use computers safely and in ways that make the world a better place.

Talk about…
Why do you think it is important to know how a computer works?

Learning outcomes: Name the main parts of a typical computer and what they are for; Say some things a computer can do and some things a computer cannot do

Class activity

Look at a computer in your classroom. Draw the computer on a big piece of paper. How many parts have you drawn? Can you name the parts? Talk to a partner about the names you know. Write the names on the drawing.

input
output   device
mouse   processor
wireless   screen

Did you know?

Computers use electricity to do their work. There are many ways to make electricity. Renewable electricity means electricity from sources that will never run out such as sunshine or wind power.

In this lesson

You will learn:

→ what a processor is

→ how computers use electricity.

Spiral back

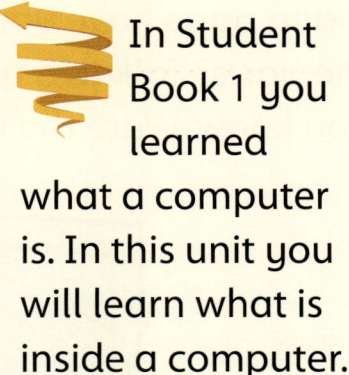

In Student Book 1 you learned what a computer is. In this unit you will learn what is inside a computer.

What is electricity?

A **device** is something people make to do a useful task. Many devices use electricity.

Electricity is a kind of energy. Wires bring electricity. The electricity flows along the wire.

But electricity is dangerous. If you touch an electric wire you will get a bad shock. It will hurt you. So be very careful with anything that has electricity in it.

Electricity ON and OFF

Electricity can be ON or OFF. Think of a light bulb. When the switch is ON, electricity can get through. The light goes on.

The OFF switch stops the electricity. The light goes off.

Inside the computer

There is an electrical device inside the computer. It is called a **processor**. The processor uses on/off electrical signals. Everything that happens inside the processor is made of on/off electrical signals.

 **Activity**

Tell a partner about the last time you used a computer. What did you use it for?

 **Extra challenge**

Draw a computer. Show the wire that brings electricity to the computer. Draw a circle where you think the processor is.

 **Think again**

What must you do to stay safe when you use electronic devices?

Inside a computer

A computer holds lots of information. For example numbers and pictures. It holds the information using electricity.

But you cannot see the electricity. The circuits are too small. It is dangerous to open a computer when the electricity is switched on.

Output devices

You cannot look at the electricity inside a computer. How can you find out what is inside the computer?

You use an **output device**.

Output devices take the electricity from the processor. They turn the electrical signals into things you can see and use.

Output you can see

The **screen** or **monitor** of a computer is an output device. It takes information from the processor. It turns it into colours and shapes.

A monitor makes visual output. That means you can see the output.

A printer gives you output. The output is on paper. You can keep the output after the computer is switched off.

Other types of output

There are other types of output.

- **Sound output:** Speakers and headphones make sound output.

- **Movement:** A computer can make a machine move. For example, a machine can clean the floor.

 **Activity**

What devices are used for output? Draw two different output devices. Write the names.

 **Extra challenge**

A 3D printer makes solid objects. For example, a 3D printer can stick blobs of plastic together. See if you can find out more.

 **Think again**

A monitor makes visual output. Say one other type of output.

1.3 Input

In this lesson

You will learn:

➔ what devices are used for input.

The user

A person who uses a computer is called the **user**. The user tells the computer what to do.

Everything inside the computer is made of electricity. How can the user put electricity into the computer?

Input devices

The answer is to use an **input device**. An input device takes a user's inputs. It turns them into electrical signals that the computer can understand.

Keyboard

A **keyboard** has keys. Touch a key. The keyboard sends a signal to the computer. It tells the computer which key you chose.

Mouse

A **mouse** can roll about on the desk. The mouse sends a signal to the computer. It tells the computer when it moves. A pointer on the screen moves about.

The mouse has a button. You click the button to make a choice.

Touchscreen

Some devices have a **touchscreen**. A touchscreen is used for input and output. It shows you choices on the screen. You touch the screen to make a choice.

Other input devices

There are other types of input. For example:

- A microphone turns sound into electric signals.
- A camera turns pictures into electric signals.

 **Activity**

What devices are used for input? Draw two different devices. Write the names.

Extra challenge

Draw a device that has a touchscreen. Show yourself in the picture using the touchscreen. What is the name of the device?

Think again What device can you use to input a song to the computer?

In this lesson

You will learn:

→ how devices are linked together.

The parts of a computer

The different devices that make a computer are called **hardware**.

The devices must be joined together.

- The input devices send signals to the processor.
- The output devices get signals from the processor.

Wired and wireless

The signals can go down wires. The signals go as electricity.

Signals can go without a wire. This is called **wireless**.

Wireless signals go through the air. They can go as radio signals. Wireless signals are safe for humans.

In the same case

Sometimes the different hardware devices are held inside the same case. The connections are hidden inside the case.

Computer networks

Computers can be joined together. The connections can be wired or wireless.

The computers can send signals to each other. This is called a computer **network**.

The **internet** is a big computer network.

 **Activity**

These pictures show things we can do using computer devices.

Draw a picture of you using a computer. Label the devices. Show the connections.

Extra challenge

Is there a network in your school? Find out more.

 **Think again** Say a device that has input and output devices in the same case.

In this lesson

You will learn:

→ what kinds of tasks computers can help us do.

What can computers do?

Mrs Harb is a teacher. She uses a computer to help with her work.

What tasks can people do by using a computer?

- Jobs where the same task is repeated over and over again, or needs to be done very carefully

- Work out hard mathematics very quickly

- Share information with lots of people all at once.

In the picture, computers are used to build cars.

Activity

Look at this picture.

Which jobs in the picture could a computer do? Which activities in the picture could a computer do? Write down your answers like this:

A computer can work out how much to charge for food.

Extra challenge

Can you think of any other everyday activities a computer could do?

Explore more

Is using a computer always the best way to carry out a task? Talk with an adult about tasks that humans do better than computers.

In this lesson

You will learn:

➜ what kinds of tasks computers cannot do easily.

What can humans do better than computers?

Humans can carry out many tasks.

I can kick a football to my friend.

Let's all take turns.

I can help my friends to stop arguing.

I can make a cup of tea.

Humans are better than computers at:

- understanding other people
- art and creativity
- inventing new ways to do things.

Activity

These girls are doing a dance. They do not want a computer to do that task. They enjoy dancing themselves.

Think of another task that humans enjoy doing. Could computers do this task instead?

Extra challenge

In a care home, old people are looked after by kind nurses. How can a computer help the nurses? What tasks are better for the nurses to do themselves?

Digital citizen of the future

Cars have been invented that can drive by themselves. They have a computer inside. Perhaps in the future nobody will drive a car. Think about the advantages and disadvantages of this. Do you want to learn to drive when you are older?

Think again Give one reason why we might decide not to use a computer to help with a task.

Check what you know

You have learned

→ what are the main parts of a computer

→ what the main parts of a computer are for

→ things computers can and cannot do.

Test

1 Draw a computer system – you can copy the example above.

2 Put these labels onto your picture.

- Keyboard
- Mouse
- Screen
- Printer

3 Show or say which parts are **input** devices. Say what input devices are used for.

4 Show or say which parts are **output** devices. Say what output devices are used for.

5 This is a tablet computer. Explain how you input to a tablet computer.

 **Activities**

1 Draw or write to show something a computer can do.

2 Draw or write to show something a computer cannot do.

3 Can you imagine something that computers might be able to do one day? Draw or write to show your idea.

Self-evaluation

- I answered test questions 1 and 2.
- I completed activity 1.
- I answered test questions 1–4.
- I completed activities 1 and 2.
- I answered all the test questions.
- I completed all the activities.

Re-read any parts of the unit you feel unsure about. Try the test and activities again – can you do more this time?

2 Digital literacy: The secret restaurant

You will learn

→ how to find useful words and images

→ how to download useful words and images

→ to explain how everyone can stay safe and happy in the computer room

→ about personal and private information and computers.

The internet lets us look at websites. The collection of all the websites in the world is called the world wide web.

You are going to use the internet to help you find delicious types of food for an imaginary secret restaurant.

 **Class activity**

Play 'whispering secrets'. Whisper a short sentence in the ear of a classmate. Your classmate then whispers what they heard to someone else. The last person says the sentence out loud.

Was the sentence the same when the last person said it out loud?

Being on the internet is like playing this game. Sometimes you will see things that are true. Sometimes you will see things that are not true, or mistakes.

browser
search engine   website
download   safe
personal information
private information
internet

Talk about...

Do you remember how to keep safe online? What can you do if you find a website that makes you feel sad or worried?

Did you know?

More than half the people in the world have access to the internet.

In this lesson

You will learn:

➜ to find out facts about foods.

Spiral back

Last year you used the internet to find things out. Now you will use those skills to find out facts about foods.

The internet

Computers all over the world are connected. All these connected computers are called the **internet**, or the world wide web.

You use a **browser** to find things on the internet. You can use a browser on a computer, on a smartphone, or on a tablet.

You can use the browser to look at **websites**. A website is a group of web pages.

You can use a **search engine** to find websites.

How to use a search engine

Open a browser by clicking twice on the browser icon on your computer.

Your teacher will help you.

Type https://www.kiddle.co/ into the address bar. The search engine will show a list of restaurants. The names are underlined. The names are links.

Type the word *restaurant* here.

Click on the name of a restaurant to open a new web page.

Every time you click on a link a new page opens.

You can go back to the page before. There is a back-arrow at the top of the browser.

Open a search engine.

Search for the type of restaurant you like best.

What kind of food is served at this type of restaurant?

- Does it serve delicious salads?
- Can you buy sweets and cakes?
- Can you buy warming soup?

What kind of imaginary secret restaurant will you have?

Extra challenge

There may be more links on the restaurant web page. Can you find them?

Think again

Tell your classmate one thing you like about the website you have found.

Tell your classmate one thing that could be improved on the website.

In this lesson

You will learn:

➜ about fact and opinion

➜ how to use a search engine.

Fact or opinion?

Say a sentence that is a fact about you. You could say, "I am 7 years old."

Say a sentence that is something you believe about yourself. This is your opinion. You could say, "I am good at running."

Sometimes you find facts on the internet. Sometimes you find opinions on the internet.

Choose websites

How can you find a book in a big library?

The internet is like a library, with websites instead of books. Search engines send software robots called 'spiders' to visit websites.

Spiders make lists of words. When you type a key word into a search engine, you are searching the big list.

These are all search engines you can use:

Type one word or a short phrase in the box on the screen.

 **Activity**

Which words do you think would be best for a search for foods at your secret restaurant?

Try out some search words of your own to find the food you like.

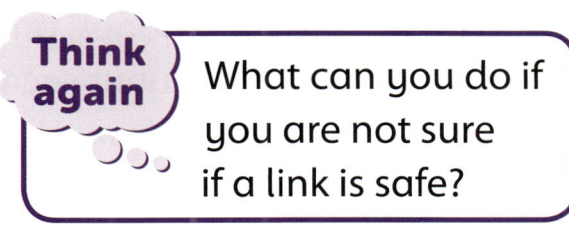

Think again

What can you do if you are not sure if a link is safe?

Extra challenge

Visit the web page of a restaurant. Find one example of a **fact** on this page. Find one example of an **opinion**.

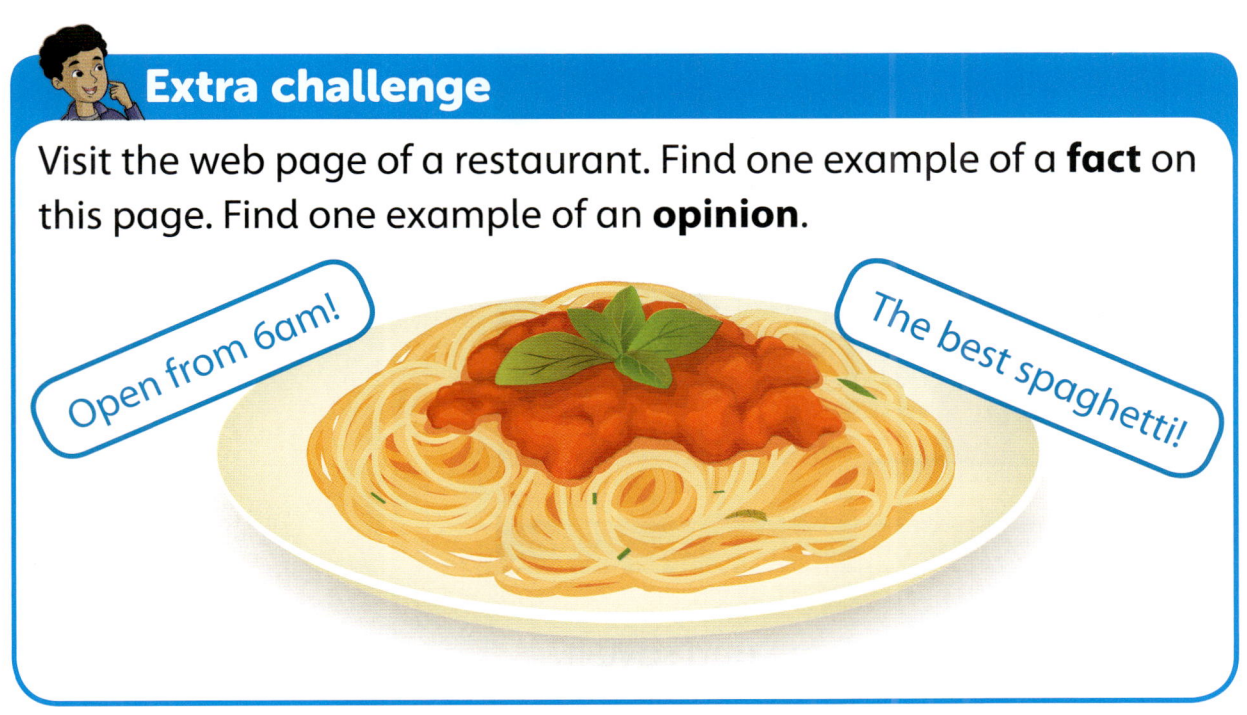

Open from 6am!

The best spaghetti!

In this lesson

You will learn:

➔ how to download words and images from the internet.

How to download images

There are fun pictures, or images, on the internet. The images would look nice on your secret restaurant menu. You can save images from the internet onto your computer. You **download** the image.

> **1** Click the right mouse button on the picture you want to download.

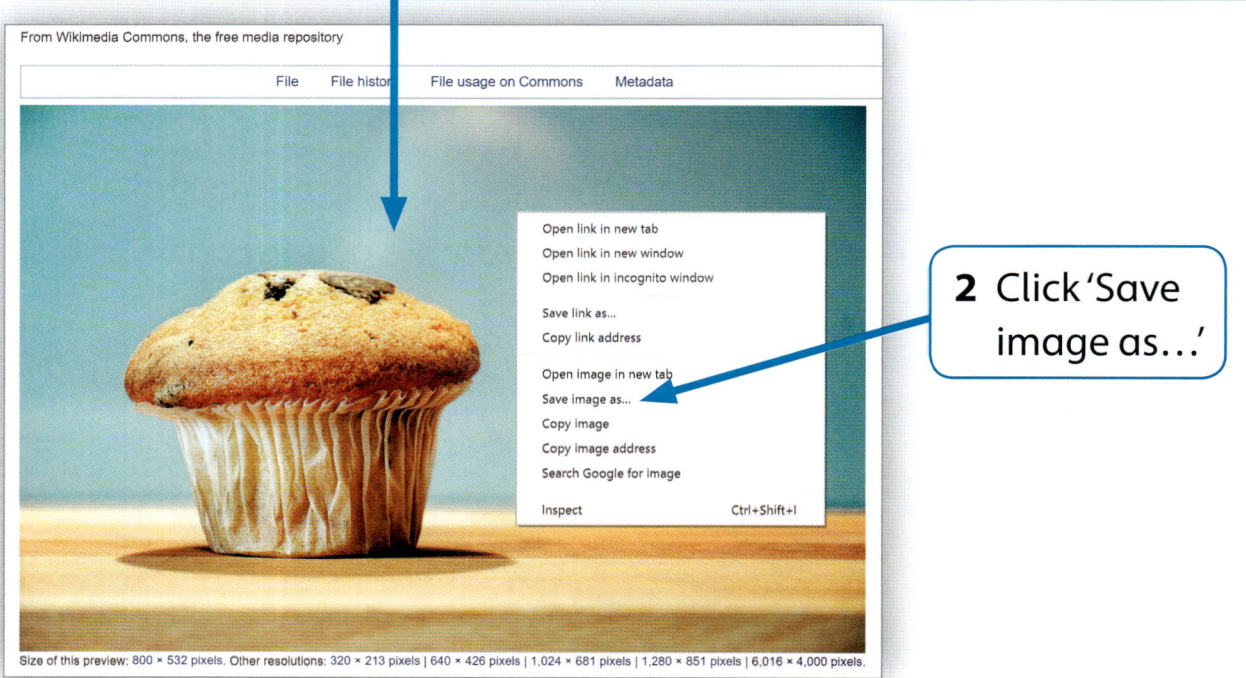

> **2** Click 'Save image as…'

Now give your image a file name and save it.

Be careful

It is wrong to steal things. You must not steal words or images from other people on the internet.

You can search for images you are allowed to download. Images you can download are 'free' images.

Use the word 'free' in your search.

The links above the line are advertisements. They are not useful.

The links below the line might be useful.

Activity

Find and save three free images of delicious-looking food from the internet.

Think again
Why is it wrong to use other people's images without their permission?

Explore more

Make a collage of your favourite foods. Find pictures of food on the internet and print them out. You can also find pictures of food in magazines or newspapers. Cut out the pictures and glue them on a piece of paper.

In this lesson

You will learn:

→   how to choose between two websites.

The three questions

This is Saima. Saima is looking at websites about food.

Saima has found a website that looks useful.

But Saima knows that some things on the internet are not true or useful.

Saima asks herself three questions.

1   Can I understand it?

2   Is it useful?

3   Can I trust it?

Saima looks at the website.

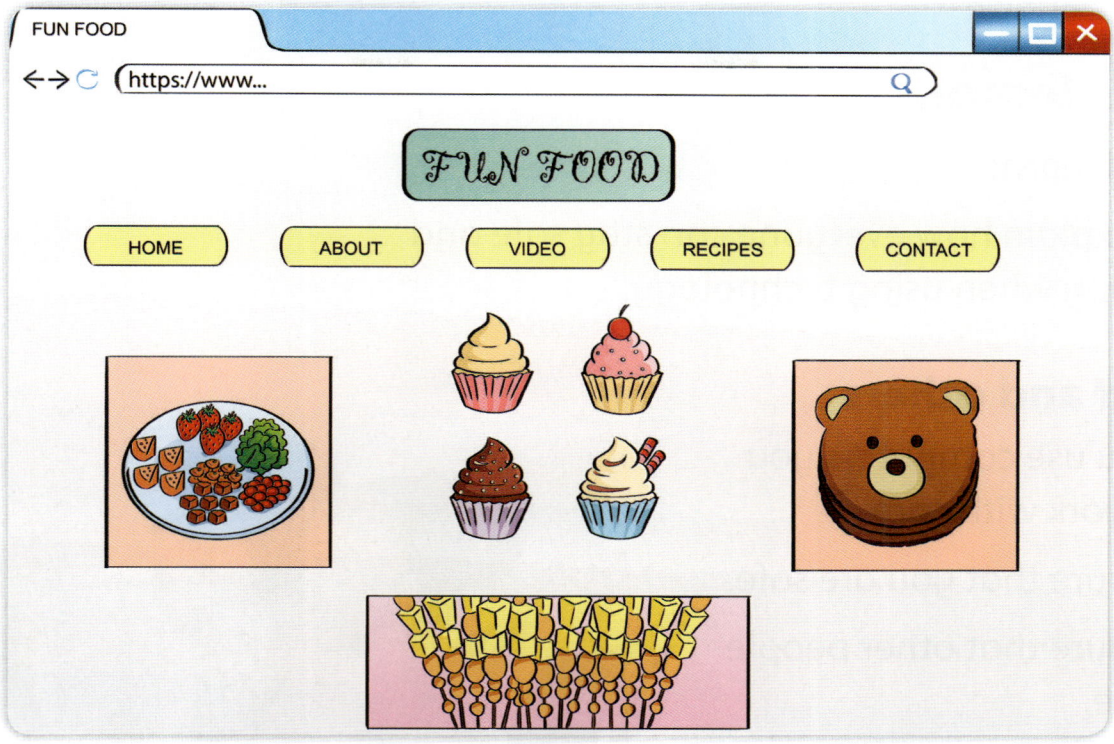

Can Saima understand the website? Saima finds some of the words difficult to understand.

Is the website useful? The images are good, and Saima knows she is allowed to download them.

Can Saima trust the website? The website shares information from experts in Australia and the UK. Saima thinks she can trust that information.

Activity

Search for a website about healthy food for children. Ask yourself the three questions about the website:

1 Can I understand it?

2 Is it useful?

3 Can I trust it?

Think again

What should you do if you are not sure if you can trust a website?

Extra challenge

As a class, make a list of easy to understand, useful, and trustworthy food websites.

2.5 Stay safe

In this lesson

You will learn:

→ to explain how everyone can stay safe and happy when using technology.

Yourself and others

When you use computers you have to work with care.

- Make sure that you are safe.
- Make sure that other people are safe.
- Do not break or spoil things.

Making choices in the classroom

Electricity is dangerous.
Computers use electricity.
Do not touch electrical wires.

Do not crowd together and push. Someone may get hurt.

Let everyone share and have their turn.

Food and drink do not belong in the computer room.

Be polite and kind.

These students are working nicely together. That makes the classroom a safe and happy place.

Making choices on the internet

In this unit you used the internet.

On the internet you can see web pages. You can type things for other people to see.

- Talk politely and kindly to others, like you do in class. Do not type angry words.

- Ask a friendly adult watch you use the internet. Ask them about anything you do not understand.

- Do not share personal information. You will find out more about this in the next lesson.

 **Activity**

Make up a short play about how to talk kindly and politely to friends online.

 **Extra challenge**

Sometimes you may spend too much time on the internet. Can you think of any ways you can help yourself remember to do other kinds of activities?

 **Explore more**

Talk to an adult about how to keep safe and happy when using computers at home.

In this lesson

You will learn:

➜ about personal and private information and computers.

In your secret restaurant you will need to keep a list of your favourite customers. You can give them treats on special days! But what information is it safe to keep about your customers?

What are personal and private information?

Personal information tells other people who you are, and where they can find you. Here are some examples of personal information:

Your name

Your address

Your favourite food

Your hobbies

Your email address

Private information is secret information about you. You must never share private information online. Here are some examples of private information.

Your password

Your date of birth   Your phone number

Information about your parents, such as their names or payment card numbers

Think again

Give an example of personal information that you would **not** share on the internet.

Activity

Look at the pictures.

Which things would you give to your family?

Which things would you give to your friends?

Which things would you give to anyone in real life?

Which things would you give to anyone on the internet?

PASSWORD

A

B

C

MY NAME

D

E

Extra challenge

Plan or draw a web page for your secret restaurant.

You have learned

→ how to find useful words and images

→ how to download useful words and images

→ to explain how everyone can stay safe and happy in the computer room

→ about personal and private information and computers.

Test

Your name is personal information.

1 Do you share personal information on the internet?

2 Give another example of personal information.

3 What would you do if someone asks you for personal information?

4 Write or draw to show how you stay safe in the classroom, and when you use the internet.

 **Activities**

1   Search safely for facts about a type of food you like. Find out:

- What are the main ingredients?
- Is it healthy food?
- Where in the world do people eat the food?

2   Download one picture from the website. Find the best picture that you can.

Self-evaluation

- I answered test question 1.
- I started activity 1 and looked at a web page.
- I worked carefully and safely.
- I answered test questions 1–3.
- I completed activity 1.
- I used the computer to help with my learning.
- I answered all the test questions.
- I completed activities 1 and 2.

Re-read any parts of the unit you feel unsure about. Try the test and activities again – can you do more this time?

3 Computational thinking: Making a good plan

You will learn

→ how to plan a program

→ what an algorithm is

→ what happens when you run a program.

In this unit you will learn to make and use a plan. A plan sets out the steps you have to take to solve a problem. Good planning can help you to achieve your goals.

 **Class activity**

Another name for the plan for a task is an algorithm.

- What is your favourite food? Do you know how to make that food? Write down the actions in the right order.

- What is your favourite computer game? Write down what happens in the game. Put the actions in the right order.

These are examples of algorithms. Make an algorithm into a poster for the classroom wall.

Learning outcomes: Say what an algorithm is and what running a program means

Talk about…

Share the recipe plans and game plans you made. Work together to make the plans even better. Can you add more actions? Can you add pictures?

Did you know?

On internet sites, such as YouTube, you can watch videos of people cooking their favourite foods.

In this lesson

You will learn:

➜ how to make a plan by choosing necessary actions.

Spiral back

Last year you used a program made of blocks. Each block stood for one action. Now you will learn to plan a program by putting actions in the right order.

The story of the donkey's hat

There was once an old lady who felt a little sad.

She made a hat for her donkey.

The old lady no longer felt sad.

Her grandson saw the donkey's hat. He asked her, "How did you do it?"

 **Activity**

Here are some actions that the old lady did that day:

| Peel the potatoes | Sew flowers on the hat | Find a straw hat |

| Pick flowers | Drink a glass of water | Tidy the room |

| Put the hat on the donkey's ears | Make holes in the hat |

Which actions are **necessary** to make the hat?
Necessary means actions that must happen.
'Tidy the room' is not necessary to make a hat.

 **Think again**
Write down the things the old lady did. Only write the ones that are necessary to make the hat.

 **Extra challenge**
Write the story of the donkey's hat in your own words. Draw a picture to go with the story.

In this lesson

You will learn:

➔ how to make a plan by putting actions in the right order.

In the last lesson you picked necessary actions to make the donkey's hat. Here are some necessary actions.

Make holes in the hat

Sew flowers on the hat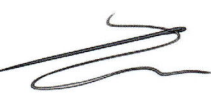

Put the hat on the donkey's ears

Pick flowers

Find a hat

Now you will put the actions in the right order.

The donkey's hat fits on the donkey's ears. But first you have to make holes, so the ears can fit.

Putting the hat on the donkey **depends** on holes for ears.

One action uses the results of the other action. That's what 'depends on' means.

So, we can tell that

Make holes in the hat

must come before

Put the hat on the donkey's ears

The right order is called the **sequence** of actions.

 **Activity**

Here are two actions:

Sew flowers on the hat

Pick some flowers

Which one has to come first? Say how you know.

 Think again Read all the actions on this page. Write the actions in the right sequence.

Extra challenge

Sometimes two actions are **independent**. That means they do not affect each other. It does not matter which comes first. What two actions in this story are independent? Say how you know.

In this lesson

You will learn:

→ what an algorithm is.

A plan that tells you how to do a task is called an **algorithm**.

The algorithm must include all the actions. The actions must be in the right order.

You can draw an algorithm. Put the actions in boxes. Join the boxes with arrows to show the right order.

Here is an algorithm for making a donkey's hat.

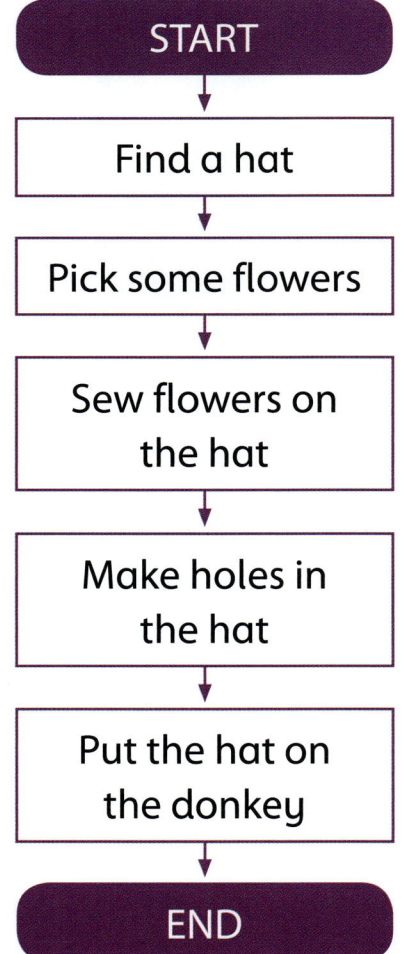

START

Find a hat

Pick some flowers

Sew flowers on the hat

Make holes in the hat

Put the hat on the donkey

END

 **Activity**

A big brother made a toy horse for his little sister. Here are the actions.

Find some wood

Carve the wood into a horse shape

Let the paint dry

Paint the horse

Buy some paint

Write the actions in the right order.

 **Extra challenge**

Make an algorithm for making a toy horse. Write the actions in boxes joined with arrows. On a big piece of paper make a colourful picture.

 **Think again**

What does 'algorithm' mean? Write or say the answer in your own words.

In this lesson

You will learn:

→ how making an algorithm helps you to plan a program.

Program

A **program** is a series of commands. The commands tell the computer what to do. When you **run a program** the computer carries out all the commands in the program.

A **programmer** is the person who makes a computer program.

A programmer sometimes makes an algorithm before they make the program. The algorithm is the plan for the program.

Sprite

You can make a program. You use a programming language to make programs. Scratch is a programming language.

- A Scratch program controls a **sprite**. A sprite is an object or creature on the screen. The program makes it do different things.

- A Scratch program is also called a **script**. A script is a short program.

 **Activity**

A programmer wanted to make a program. The sprite is a penguin. Here is a list of things that the penguin will do.

Say goodbye

Go off the screen

Say hello and your name

Ask your name

Come onto the screen

Put these actions in the right order.

Think again Write an algorithm showing the actions of the program in boxes joined by arrows.

Extra challenge

Think of one extra action the penguin could do. Make a plan for the program that includes the extra action.

Be creative

Plan a new computer program:

- Draw the sprite.
- Say what actions the sprite will do.

In this lesson

You will learn:

➜ how to plan a program called the Frog Hop Game.

Program actions

A student decided to make a computer game.

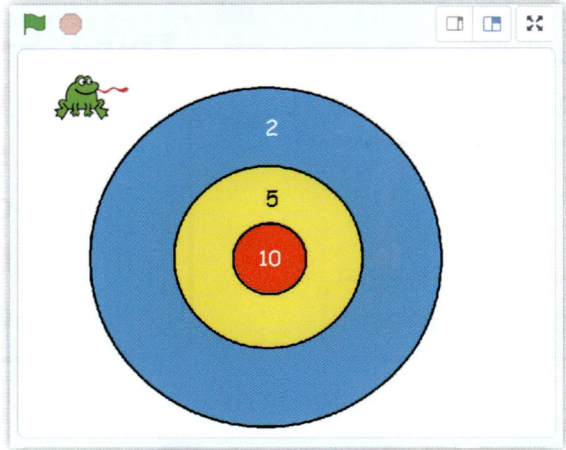

First he wrote down what the game would do.

> *The sprite is a frog. The background is a target. When you click on the frog it jumps to a new place on the target. You get points depending on where the frog jumps.*

Here are the actions of the program:

The frog jumps to a place on the target

The user clicks the frog

The frog says how many points you got

Work out how many points you get

 **Activity**

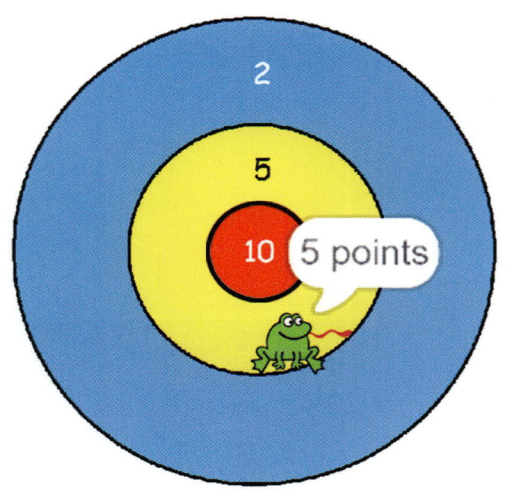

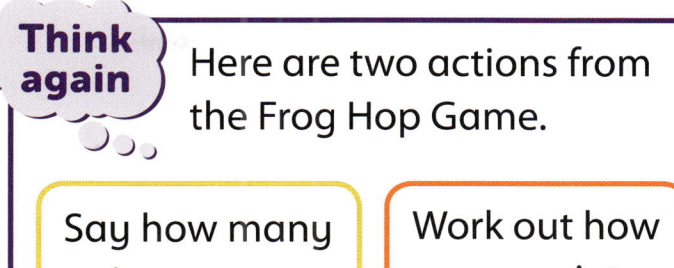

Think again Here are two actions from the Frog Hop Game.

| Say how many points | Work out how many points |

One action must come before the other. Which one comes first? Give a reason for your answer.

Put the actions in the right order.

Make an algorithm.

Extra challenge

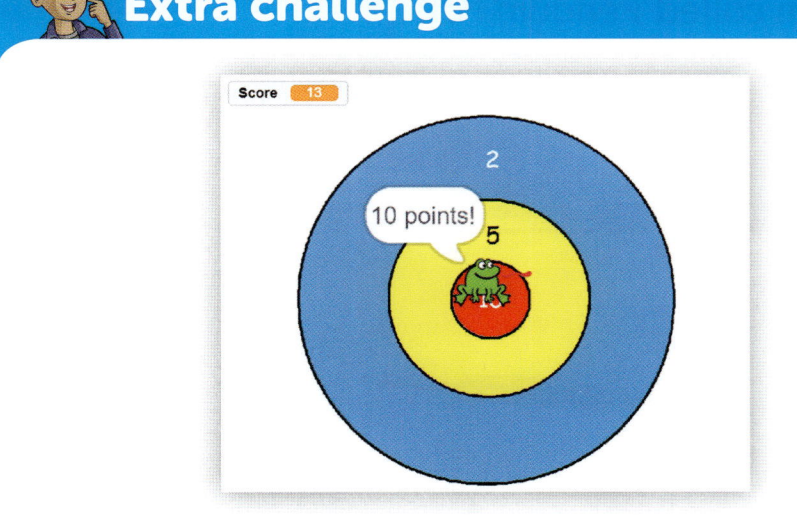

The student wanted to change the program like this.

- Start with total score 0.
- When you get points add to your total score.
- See the total score at the end of the game.

Make an algorithm that includes these new actions.

In this lesson

You will learn:

➜ how to run a program.

Load the program

There is a ready-made program for you to **run**. 'Run a program' means the computer carries out the commands in the program.

First you must **load** the program. Loading means getting a program from storage. The penguin pal program is stored on your computer.

Open the file menu. Click on 'Load from your computer'. Choose the program called 'Penguin Pal'.

The Scratch screen

You will see a screen like this:

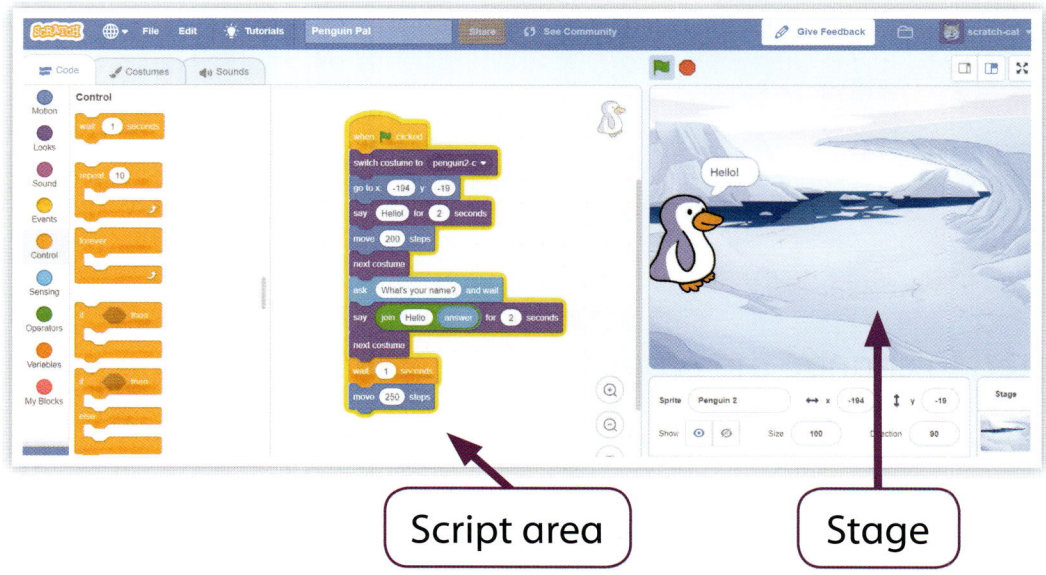

Can you see the **script area**? The script area shows the program.

Can you see the **stage**? The stage is where the sprite moves.

Run the program

Every program script starts with an **'Event' block**. This program starts with a block that shows a green flag. Click on the green flag. This will start the program.

  **Activity**

Load and run the penguin program.

Extra challenge

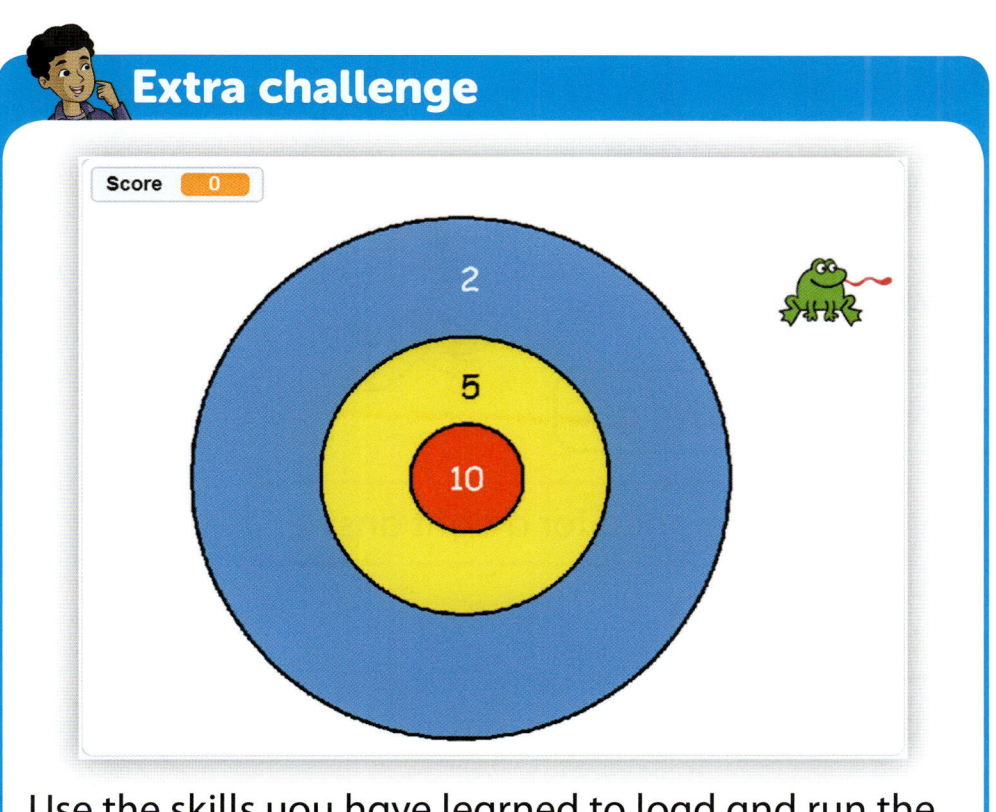

Score 0

2

5

10

 Use the skills you have learned to load and run the Frog Hop program.

 **Explore more**

Tell your family about the Frog Hop Game. If you get a chance, play the game with your friends at school. Ask everyone what they like best about the game. Ask them what could be better. Note down their answers.

Check what you know

You have learned

→ how to plan a program

→ what an algorithm is

→ what happens when you run a program.

 **Activity**

Here is a plan for the actions in a quiz program. They are not sorted into order.

> What is the tallest mountain in the world?

Tell you if the answer is right

Show how many points you have got

Ask a question

Give you a point for a right answer

Get the answer to the question

Make an algorithm by putting the actions in the right order.

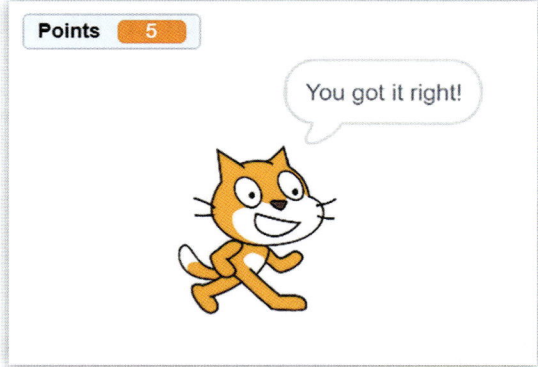

Points 5

> You got it right!

Test

A programmer made a program. Here are the three things she did.

Plan the program
Write the program
Run the program

1 Write the three actions in your book.

2 Tick the action that means carry out the commands.

3 Put a star next to the one that means make an algorithm.

4 Fill in the missing words in these sentences. Use the words from the box.

> actions   algorithm   sequence   program

An _____ is a plan to make a _____.

It sets out all the _____ in the right _____.

Self-evaluation

- I answered test questions 1 and 2.

- I answered test questions 1–3.

- I did some of the activity.

- I answered all the test questions.

- I did all of the activity.

Re-read any parts of the unit you feel unsure about. Try the test and activities again – can you do more this time?

4 Programming: The Frog Hop Game

You will learn

→ how a program is made of commands

→ how to pick commands to make the program you want

→ how to make a program that works

→ how to make changes and corrections to a program.

In this unit you will make a computer program. You will make a new computer game called the Frog Hop Game. You will use Scratch.

 **Class activity**

Here is a picture of the Scratch screen:

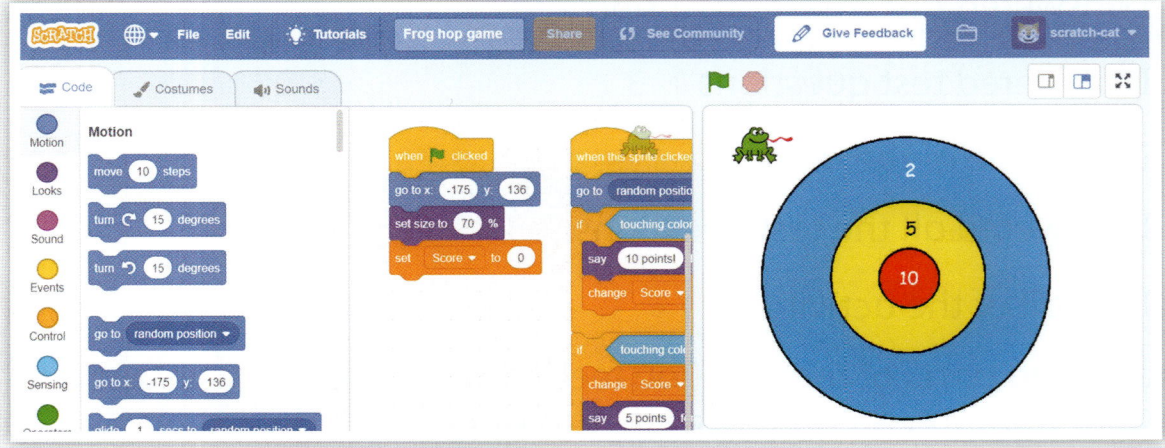

Learning outcomes: Say what a program will do by looking at its commands; Create a simple program and remove errors so it runs

The different parts of the screen are:

- the code blocks: the blocks are stored here ready to use
- the script area: this is where you make a program
- the stage: this is where the sprite moves
- the menu bar: you can choose commands from here.

Point to the different parts of the screen.

Draw the Scratch screen. Write the names of the different parts of the screen.

> user   event
> command   forever loop
> random location

Talk about...

In this unit you will save your work. You must choose a file name. What makes a good file name? Talk to a classmate, then share your ideas with the rest of the class.

Did you know?

Scratch is used by children in more than 150 different countries. Scratch is available in different languages. You can make Scratch programs in more than 40 different languages.

In this lesson

You will learn:

→ how to choose a sprite for your program.

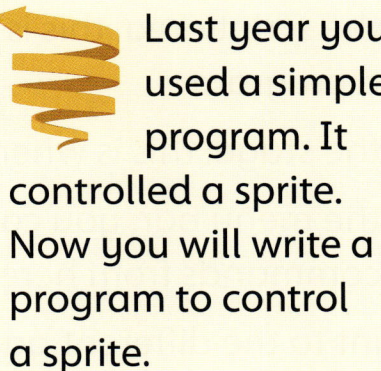

Last year you used a simple program. It controlled a sprite. Now you will write a program to control a sprite.

In Unit 3 you played the Frog Hop Game. In this unit you will make a simple version of the game. You can choose any sprite you like. It does not have to be a frog.

You will make a Scratch program. Start on the Scratch website.

Choose a sprite

Look at the bottom right. This part of the screen shows the sprites.

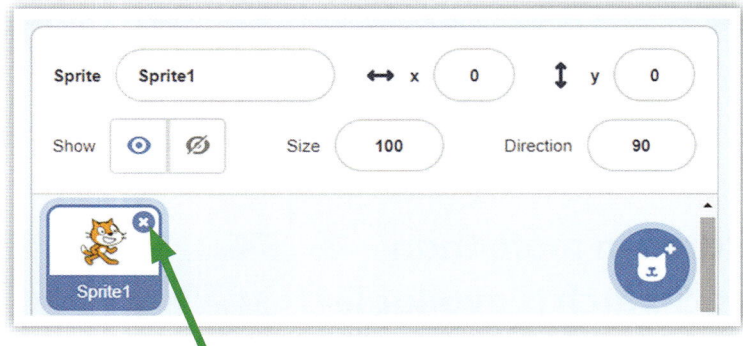

Sprite 1 is a cat. Delete this sprite by clicking on the cross.

You will choose a new sprite.

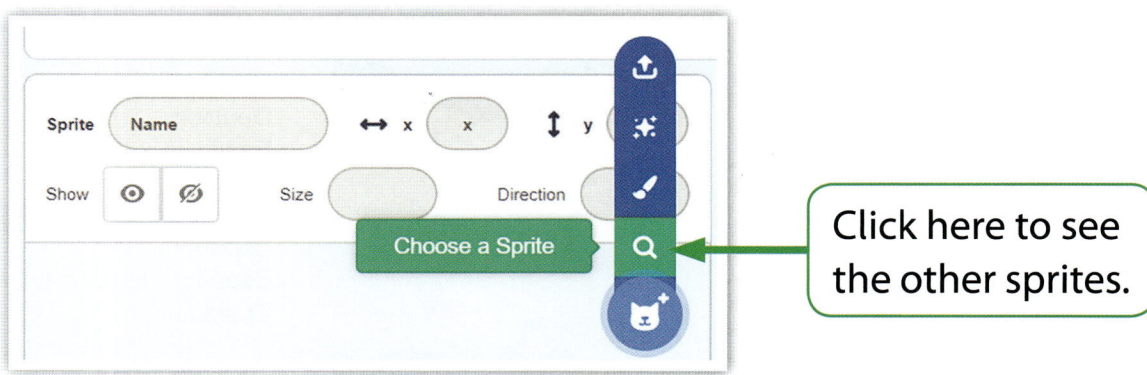

Click here to see the other sprites.

You will see pictures of sprites.

Click on the one you choose.

Save program file

Now you must save your work. You will save it on your computer. Open the File menu and choose 'Save to your computer'. Then type a name for your file.

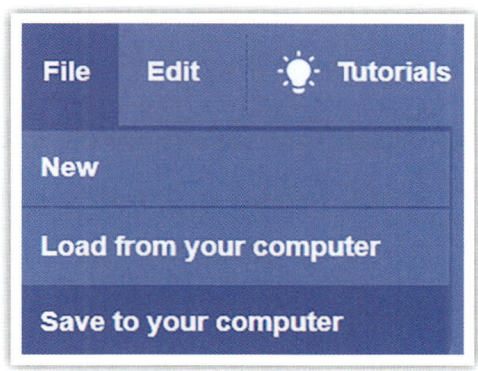

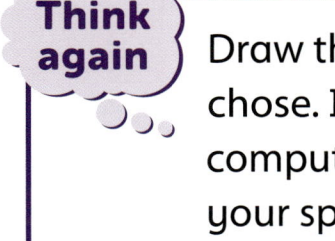 **Activity**

Use the skills you learned to:

- pick a sprite
- save your file.

Think again Draw the sprite you chose. Imagine a computer game with your sprite in it. Write down your idea.

Extra challenge

Add a backdrop to your program.

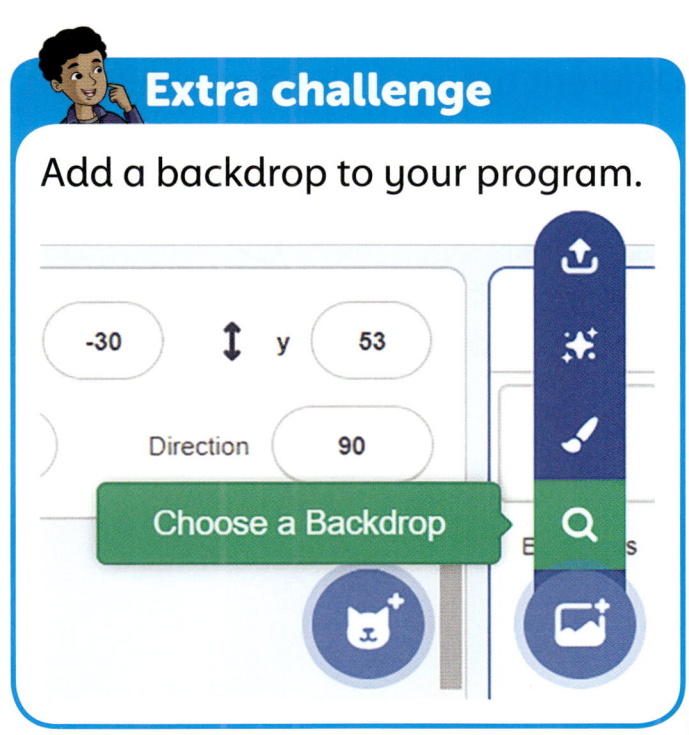

4.2 Command your sprite

In this lesson

You will learn:

→ how to add commands to your program.

Load program file

Last lesson you saved your work as a file. Now you will load the file. Load means get a file from storage.

Open the file menu. Click on 'load from your computer'. Choose the file you made last time.

Coloured dots and blocks

You will make a Scratch program. A program is made of **commands**. Commands tell the computer what to do.

Scratch commands are blocks. You fit the blocks together. That makes the program.

Different types of blocks are different colours.

● 'Motion' blocks are blue.

● 'Sound' blocks are pink.

Look for the coloured dots on the left of the screen. Choose a colour to help you pick the blocks you need.

Actions

Choose a block. It will make your sprite move.

Click on the blue dot. You will see 'Motion' blocks.

Find the block that says 'go to random position'.

Drag this block to the middle of the screen.

Click on the block. The sprite will move.

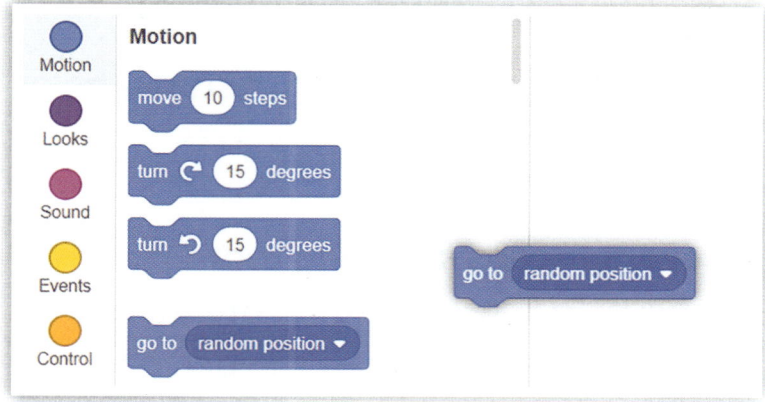

Sounds

Choose a block. It will play a sound. Click on the pink dot. You will see 'Sound' blocks. Choose the 'play sound' block.

Now you have two blocks. Fit the blocks together.

Click on the two blocks. What happens?

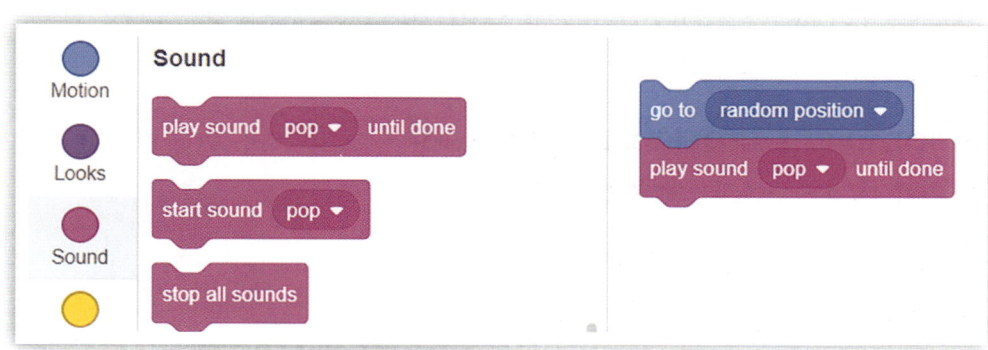

 **Activity**

Make the two-block program shown on this page.

 **Extra challenge**

Add any other block to the program. See what happens when you run the program.

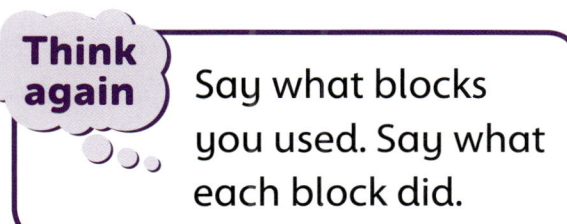 **Think again** Say what blocks you used. Say what each block did.

In this lesson

You will learn:

→ to choose an event that starts the program.

Events

An **event** means anything that happens. In Scratch 'Events' are things the **user** does. The user is the person who uses the program. Now you will choose the 'Event' that lets the user start your program.

Click on the yellow dot that says 'Events'.

What 'Event' blocks can you see? What does each one say?

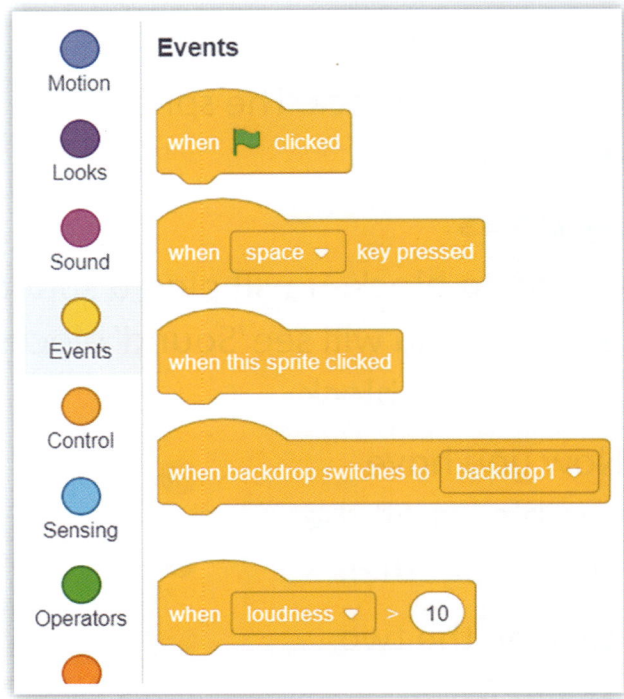

Choose an event

To choose an 'Event' drag the block to the program area.

Find the 'Event' block that says 'when this sprite clicked'.

Fit the program blocks onto the 'Event' block. Now the event will start the program.

Change colour

Now you will make the sprite change colour. Click on the purple dot that says 'Looks'. These command blocks change the look of the sprite.

Find the block that says 'change color effect by…'.

Drag this block to the script area and add it to the program.

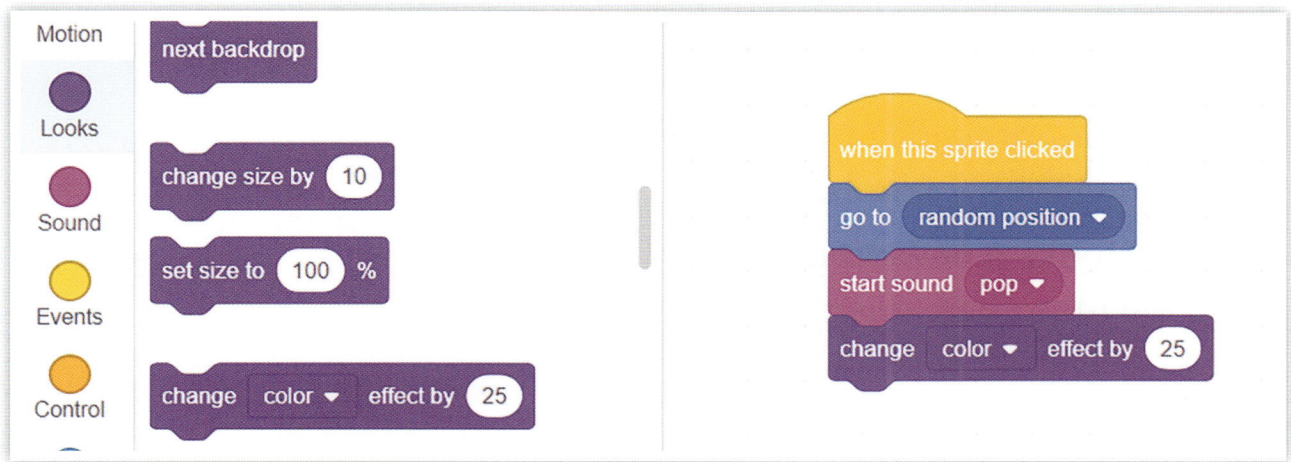

 **Activity**

Change your program.

- Add the 'Event' block which says 'when this sprite clicked'.

- Add the 'Looks' block which changes the colour of the sprite.

Click the sprite to make it move.

Save the file.

 **Extra challenge**

Choose a different start event. Change the program to the new event.

 **Think again**

Draw the 'Event' block you used. Say what it does.

If you used more than one, draw them all.

In this lesson

You will learn:

→ how to change the program so the sprite moves 'forever'.

Last lesson you wrote a program. The program started when you clicked on the sprite. The sprite moved to a new place. The sprite made a sound. These things happened one time.

Now you will make a new program. In this program the sprite will move over and over again. The action will repeat.

New program

Open the file menu. Click on 'New' to make a new program.

Control blocks

Click on the orange button. You will see the orange 'Control' blocks. Find the block that says 'forever'. This block is called the **forever loop**. Drag it to the middle of the screen.

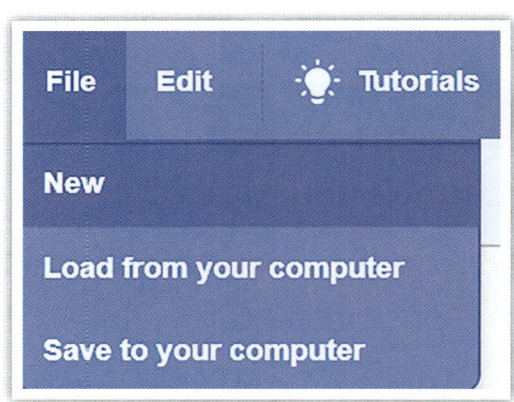

A forever loop is a way to control the program. Commands inside the forever loop will repeat.

Add commands

Here are the commands you want to repeat:

● Make the sound 'pop'.

● Go to a random position.

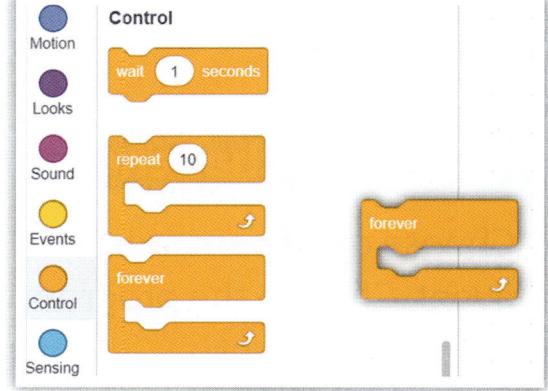

Put these blocks inside the forever loop. They are the same blocks you used in the last program.

Wait

Add one more block inside the forever loop. You will find it with the orange control blocks. It says 'wait 1 seconds'. This will make the sprite wait for 1 second between jumps.

The completed program looks like this.

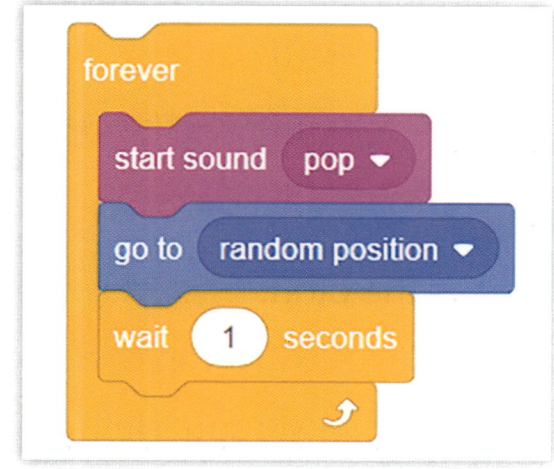

 **Activity**

Start a new program. Choose a sprite and a background.

Make the program shown on this page. Run the program to see what happens.

 **Think again** Say what happens when you put blocks inside a forever loop.

Extra challenge

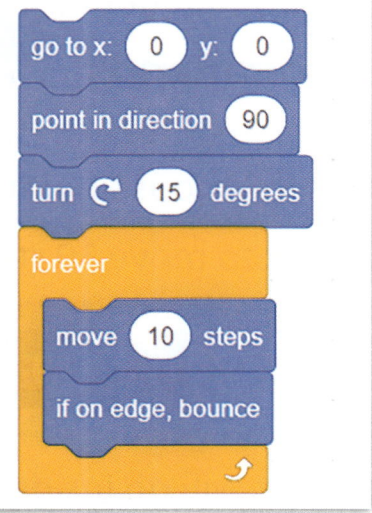

Here is a new program that uses the forever loop.

- Make this program.
- Add a start 'Event' to the program.
- Change the numbers in the program and see what happens.

In this lesson

You will learn:

→ how to make a new program to match a plan.

Plan

Here is the plan.

- The sprite will jump to a random place.
- The sprite will say "Hello!"
- The sprite will keep moving towards the mouse pointer.

First commands

The sprite will start in a **random** place. Random means you do not know where it will go.

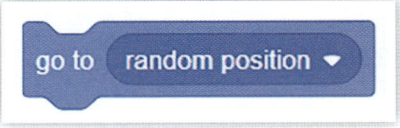

The sprite will say "Hello!"

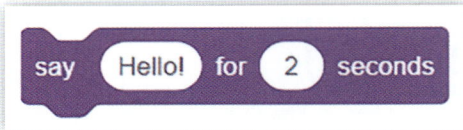

Find these blocks and fit them together.

Repeated commands

Here is the block that makes the sprite point towards the mouse pointer.

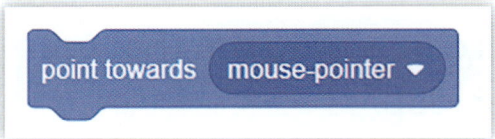

Here is the block to move 10 steps.

These two blocks will go inside a forever loop.

Completed program

Here is the program with all the pieces in place. It has a start 'Event' – the green flag.

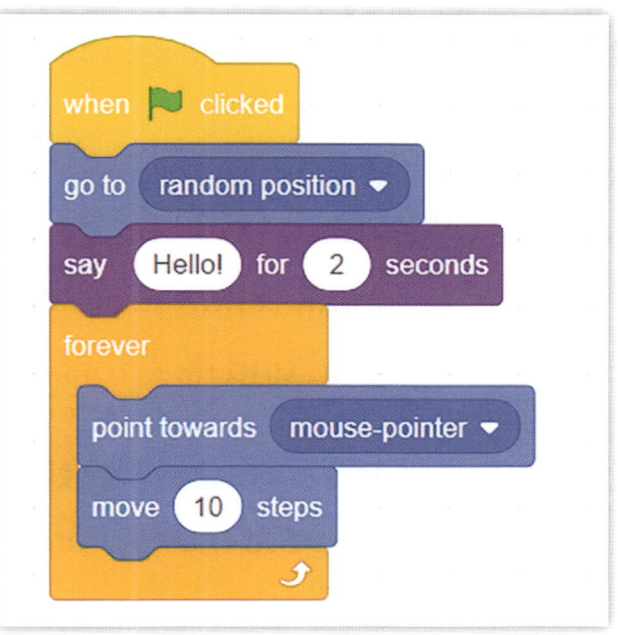

 **Activity**

Start a new program. Choose a sprite that looks like a fish. Choose a background that looks like underwater.

Make the program shown on this page. The program will make the fish swim about underwater.

Think again

Think of one change you could make to the program you made. What would happen if you made this change?

Extra challenge

Add a jellyfish sprite to the underwater scene. Make a program for this sprite.

- Use the same blocks as before.
- Take out the block that says 'follow the mouse pointer'.
- Add a block that says 'if on edge bounce'.
- Make the number of steps 2 instead of 10.

In this lesson

You will learn:

➔ how to make changes to a program

➔ how to find and fix errors.

Commands to match actions

A student wanted to make a program. They decided the sprite would:

● jump to a random place

● say "Hello!"

● move around the screen forever.

The student found blocks to match the actions. Here is the program made of those blocks.

The student ran the program. The program did not work the way they wanted. The sprite moved just once, then stopped.

Using a loop

The student decided to use a 'forever loop'. They put all the command blocks inside the loop. Here is the program they made.

The student ran the program. The program did not work the way they wanted. Too many blocks are inside the loop. The sprite keeps jumping to a new place. The sprite keeps saying "Hello!"

Inside and outside the loop

Some commands should go before the loop. Those are the commands that must happen only once.

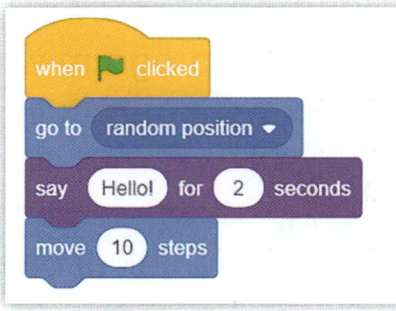

Some commands should be put inside the loop. Those are the commands that will be repeated.

Look at the final picture on the previous page. You will see the program with all the commands in the right place.

Add some bounce

The sprite moves until it is almost off the screen and then stops. You must add a block that tells the sprite to 'bounce' if it hits the side.

The finished program is shown here.

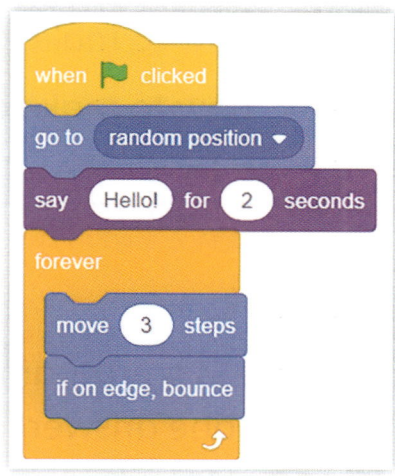

Using the ideas on this page make a program that makes a butterfly move about the screen.

Extra challenge

Look in the program you made to find the block that says 'move 10 steps'.

Change the number. Run the program and see what is different.

Explore what happens when you use different numbers.

Explore more

Make a new program. Use a sprite that looks like a ball. Make it bounce around the screen.

Add different types of ball. Set them to different speeds.

Check what you know

You have learned

→ how a program is made of commands

→ how to pick commands to make the program you want

→ how to make a program that works

→ how to make changes and corrections to a program.

Test

Here is a program made using Scratch. Pick one answer for each question.

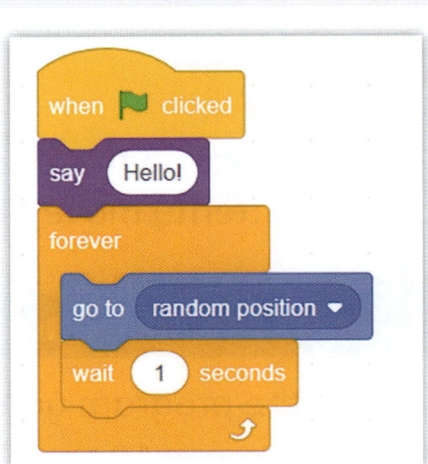

1 What does this program do?

   a Make the sprite move about.

   b Click the green flag.

   c Play a game.

2 What happens at the start of the program?

   a The sprite moves forward 10 steps.

   b The sprite says "Hello!"

   c The sprite goes to a random position.

3 What commands will be repeated?

   a The sprite asks your name and says "Hello!" to you.

   b The sprite points towards the mouse and moves forward.

   c The sprite goes to a random place and waits 1 second.

4 If you add this block inside the forever loop what will happen?

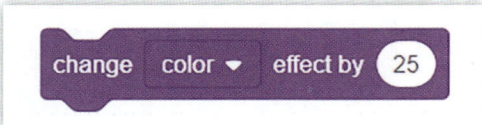

a The sprite changes colour once.

b The sprite changes colour lots of times.

c The sprite changes colour to red.

Activities

1 Make a program that does this:

- The sprite walks forward 10 steps.
- The sprite says "Goodbye!"
- The sprite walks another 10 steps.

2 Plan and make a program that has a forever loop in it. You can decide what commands to put in your program.

Self-evaluation

- I answered test question 1 and started activity 1.
- I answered test questions 1–3. I completed activity 1.
- I answered all the test questions. I completed both activities.

Re-read any parts of the unit you feel unsure about. Try the test and activities again – can you do more this time?

5 Multimedia My hobbies

You will learn

→ how to make a document with words

→ how to make a document with pictures

→ how to save work as a file

→ how to open a saved file.

What is your name?

What do you like to do for fun?

In this unit you will use words and pictures to make a page about your favourite hobby.

Talk about...

We all have something we are good at. We call things we are good at our 'talents'. What is your talent?

Tell a classmate about your talent.

Learning outcomes: Make a document with words and pictures; Save your work as a file in storage

Class activity

Your teacher will give you a strip of paper and a pencil.

Write about or draw something you are good at on your paper.

Put glue on the end of your paper. Link all of your papers together like this.

document   images
save   file   text box
border

Decorate your class with your talent paper garland!

Did you know?

Something you do for fun can help you to feel relaxed and happy.

In this lesson

You will learn:

→ to make a poster with pictures and words

→ to save your page so you can use it later.

Hobbies

Oliver enjoys reading. His favourite hobby is reading.

Ava enjoys skipping. Her favourite hobby is skipping.

What is your favourite hobby?

You will find out how Oliver makes a poster about his hobby.

You will make a page about your favourite hobby

Add a title to your poster

Oliver's favourite hobby is reading. He adds a title to his poster. The title is, 'My hobby is reading'. He types the title using his keyboard.

1 Oliver types a heading. Letters appear on screen at the cursor.

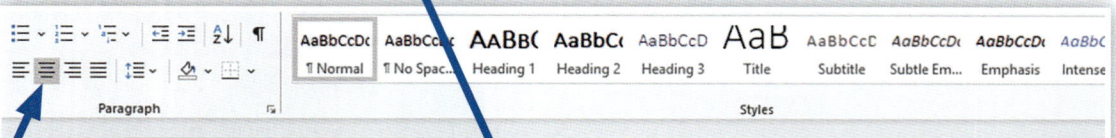

2 Oliver clicks the button to move his title to the centre of the screen.

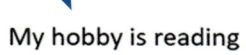

My hobby is reading

Oliver has started his poster. He does not want to lose his poster. He wants to work on it again later. Oliver needs to save his poster.

Save your work

A file is a place to keep information on a computer. Oliver saves his work in a file.

He clicks 'File'. He clicks 'Save As'.

He calls the file, 'My hobby'.

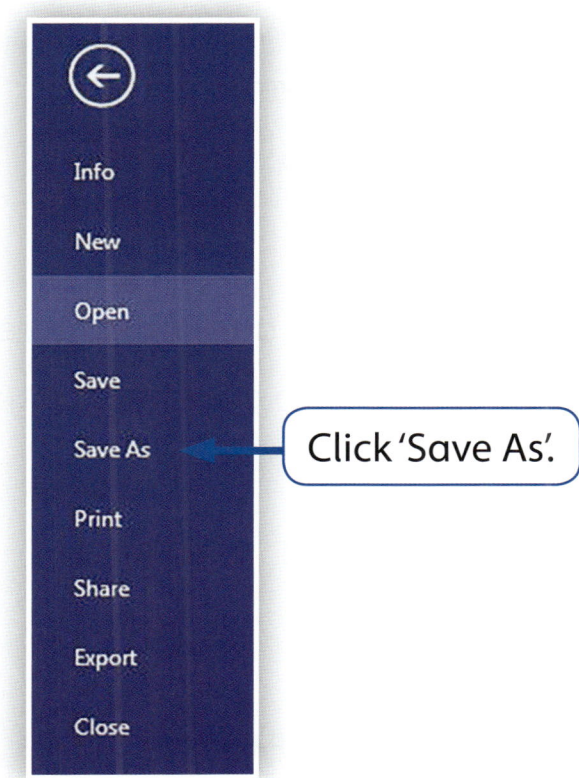

Click 'File'.

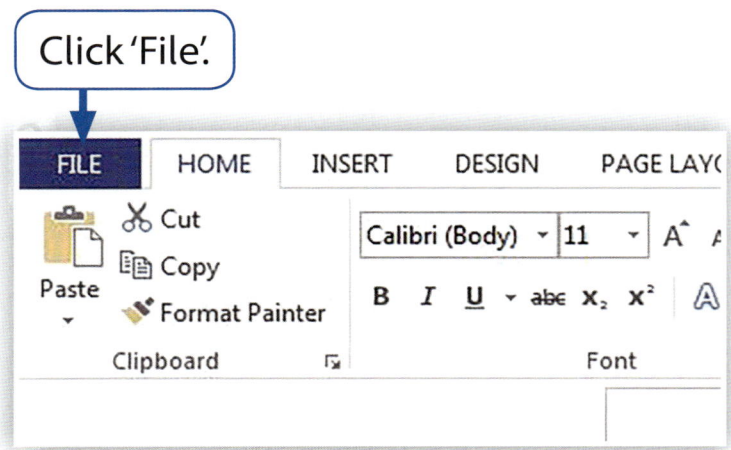

Click 'Save As'.

Activity

Choose your favourite hobby. Open a new document on your computer. Type a heading for your poster. Type your heading in the same way Oliver did.

Think again

- What do you like about your hobby?
- What is difficult about your hobby?
- Does your hobby use special equipment?

Make some notes about your hobby. You can use them later when you add words to your poster.

Extra challenge

Save your work in a file called 'My hobby'.

In this lesson

You will learn:

→ how to open a saved file

→ how to add a text box.

Open a file

You are going to add some more words to your poster.

First, you need to open the file you saved in the last lesson.

Click 'File'.

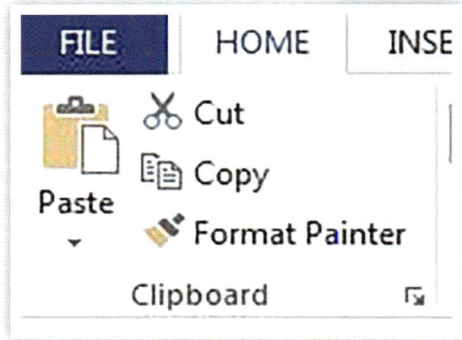

Click 'Open'.

Click the name of file you want to open.

Add a text box

Word-processing applications let you put words and pictures together. You can put the words into a rectangle shape anywhere on the page. The rectangle shape is called a **text box**.

1 Click 'Insert'.

2 Click 'Text Box'.

3 Choose 'Simple Text Box'.

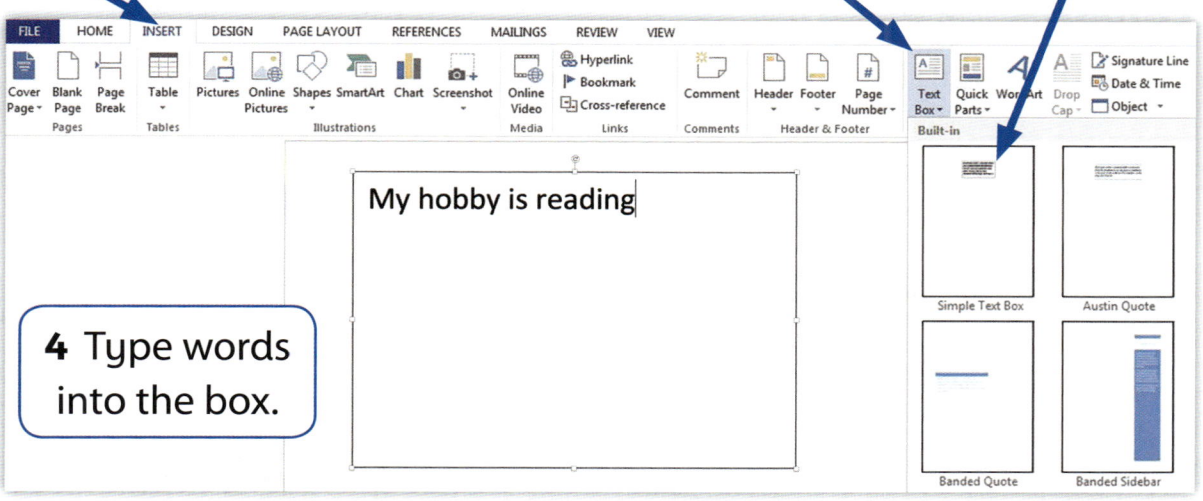

4 Type words into the box.

My hobby is reading

 **Activity**

Add a text box to your file about your favourite hobby. Write about your favourite hobby.

- What is your favourite hobby?
- Why do you like your hobby?
- What is difficult in your hobby?
- What is easy in your hobby?

 Extra challenge

Can you move the text box to a different place on the screen?

Can you change the colour of the text in the box?

 **Explore more**

Look at signs and posters near your home. How big are the words and pictures? Why do you think the poster looks that way?

In this lesson

You will learn:

➜ how to add images to your poster.

Find images

Some programs can help you find pictures, or images.

1 Click 'Insert'.

2 Click 'Online Pictures'.

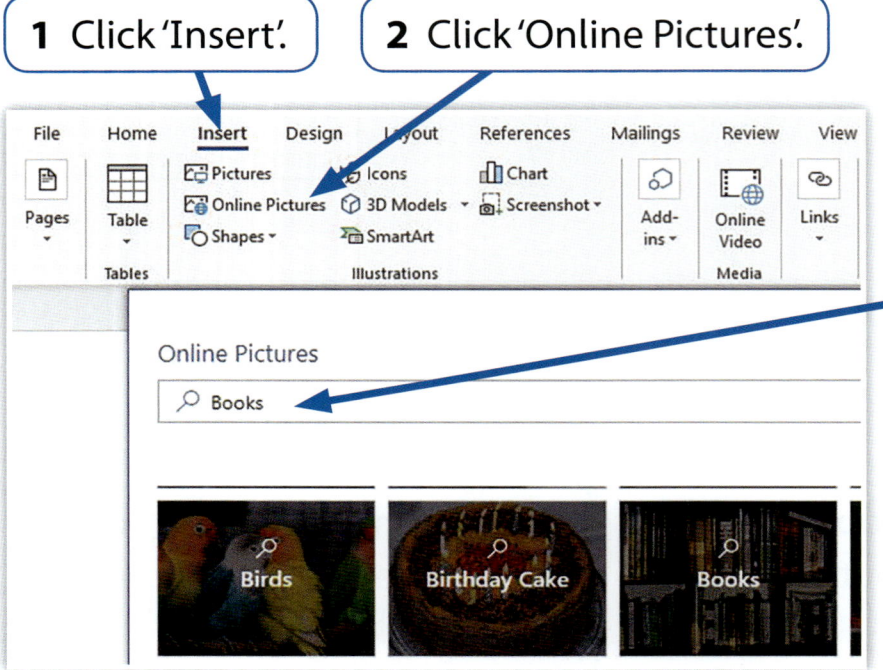

3 Type a search term here. Press 'Enter'.

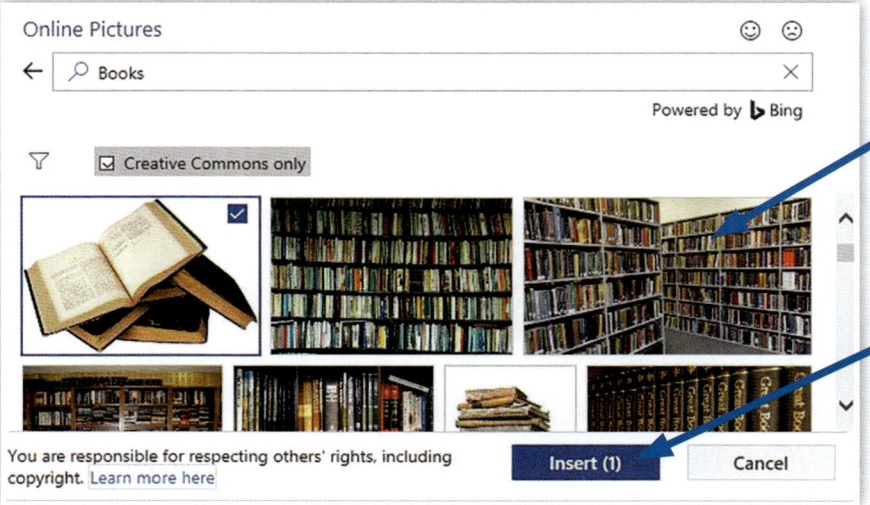

1 Choose an image you like.

2 Click 'Insert'.

 **Activity**

Open your 'My hobby' file.

Search for an image that says something about your hobby. Insert the image into your poster.

Save your file.

Think again Why did you like the image you chose the best?

Extra challenge

Change the way your poster title looks.

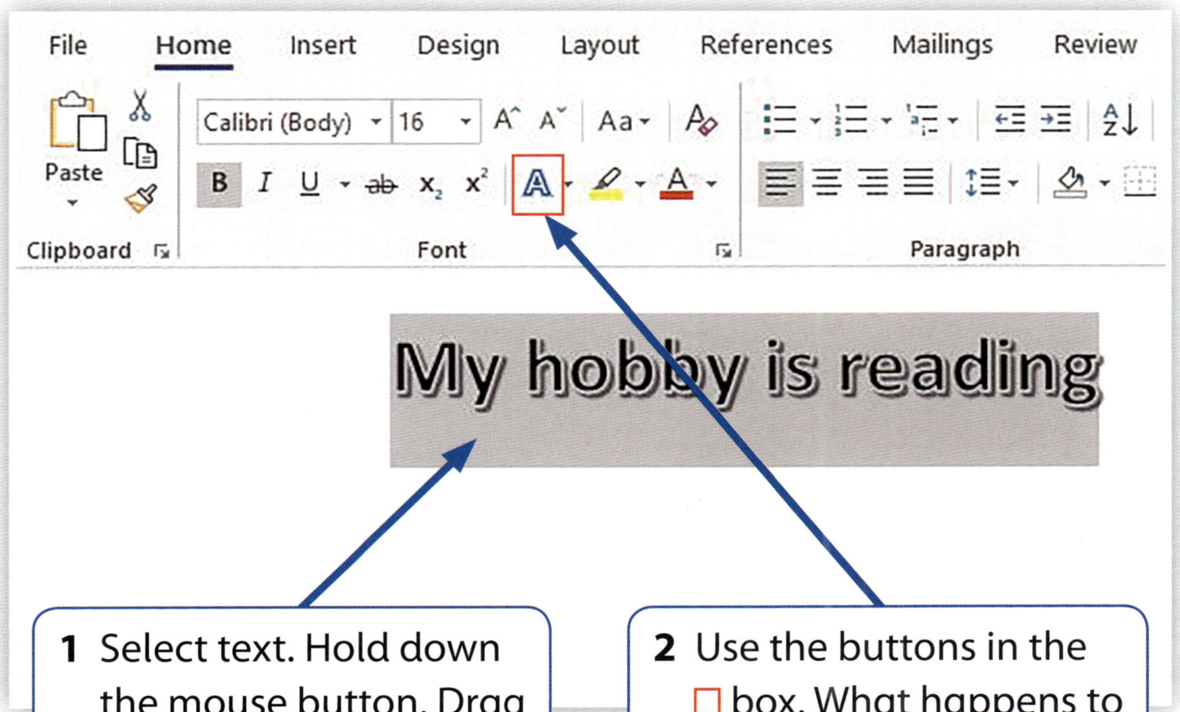

| File | Home | Insert | Design | Layout | References | Mailings | Review |

Calibri (Body) ▾ 16 ▾ | A˄ A˅ | Aa▾ | A

B I U ▾ ab x₂ x² | **A** ▾ 🖊 ▾ A ▾

Clipboard   Font   Paragraph

My hobby is reading

1 Select text. Hold down the mouse button. Drag over the text so that all the text is shaded.

2 Use the buttons in the ☐ box. What happens to your poster title?

In this lesson

You will learn:

→ how to move images on a page

→ how to make images smaller or larger.

Oliver has put an image of books into his poster. He wants to move the image to the bottom of the poster.

How to move an image

Click on the image that you want to move.

1 Click this button.

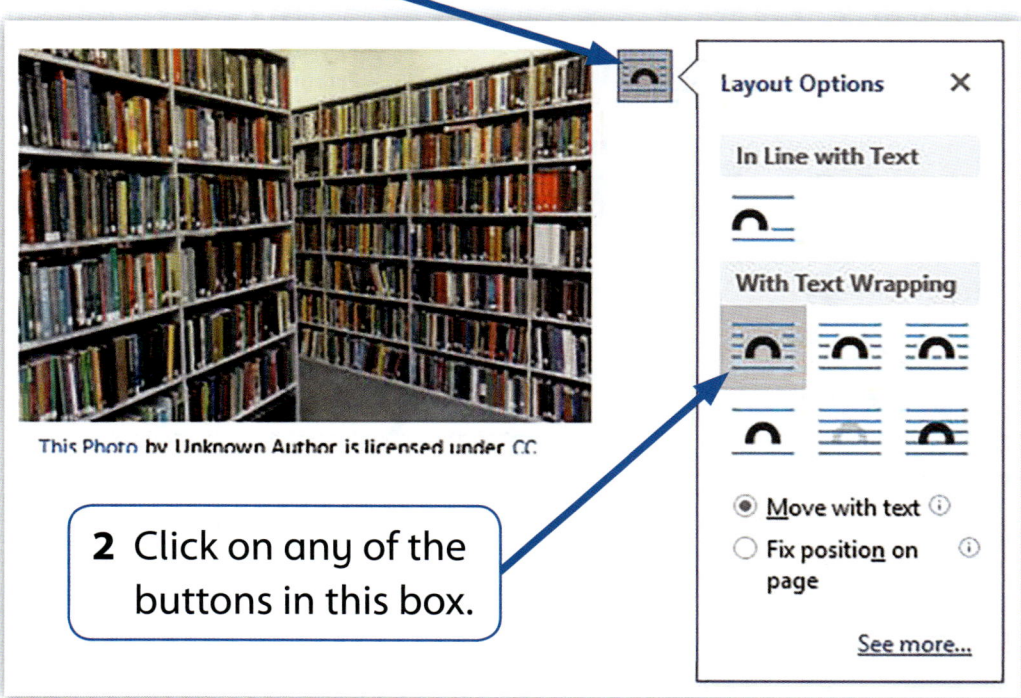

This Photo by Unknown Author is licensed under CC.

2 Click on any of the buttons in this box.

Now you can move the image. Click and hold your mouse button anywhere over the image. Drag the image where you want to move it to. Release the mouse button.

Change the size of an image

You can change the size of image. You can make the image smaller or larger.

Click on the image. A box appears around the image. Click and hold your mouse button over one corner of the box.

Make the image smaller. Drag your mouse towards the middle of the image. Make your image larger. Drag your mouse away from the middle of the image.

This Photo by Unknown Author is licensed under CC.

 **Activity**

Open your file called 'My hobby'.

Change the size of the image in your poster.

Move the image to the middle of the page.

Save your file.

Extra challenge

Find a second image to add to your poster. Place the two images on your poster.

Think again Would you prefer to add one large image or many small images to your poster? Give reasons for your choice.

In this lesson

You will learn:

→ how to add shapes as text boxes.

Shape text boxes

You have learned how to add a text box. You can put your text anywhere on a page using text boxes.

You can also add text in shapes to make your work more exciting and fun.

Choose a text box shape

1 Click 'Insert'.

2 Click 'Shapes'. Choose a shape.

3 Drag the shape to the right size and place.

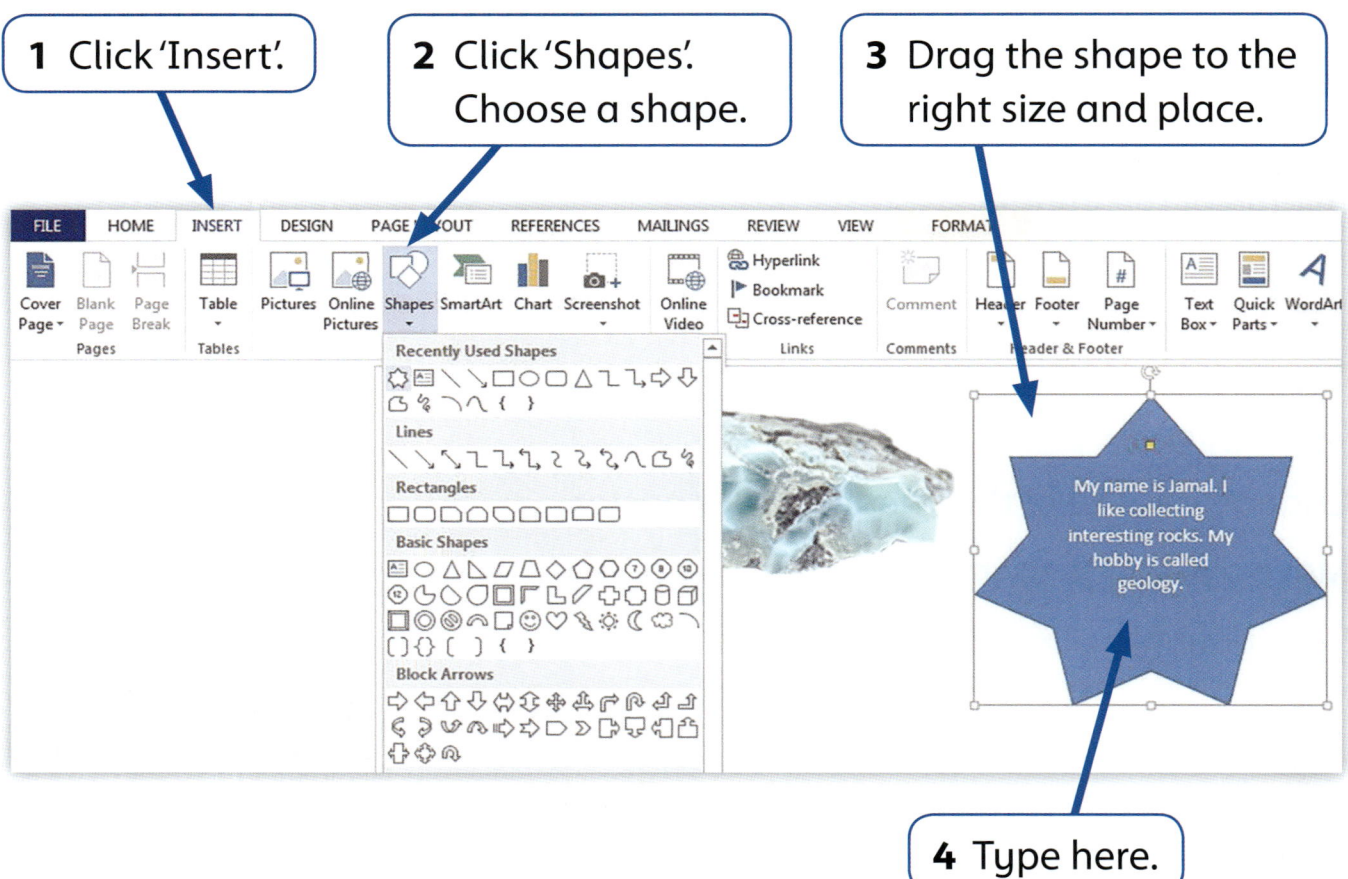

4 Type here.

Change the look of a text box

First click on the shape.

1 Click 'Format'.

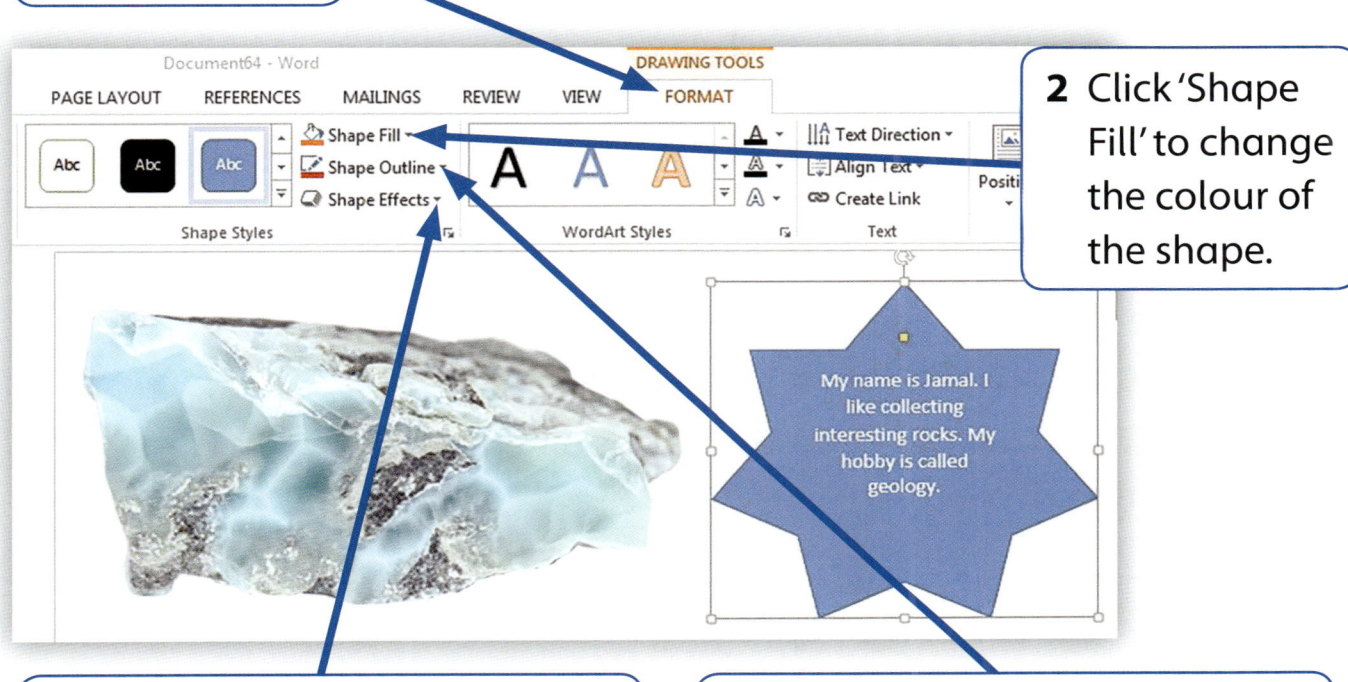

2 Click 'Shape Fill' to change the colour of the shape.

4 Click 'Shape Effects' to make the shape edge look different.

3 Click 'Shape Outline' to change the colour of the shape border.

 **Activity**

Open your file called 'My hobby'.

Add a shape to your poster. Add an important message inside the shape. For example, have you made friends doing your hobby? Make the box look the way you want.

Save your file.

Think again Why could it be useful to have your text in a different shape?

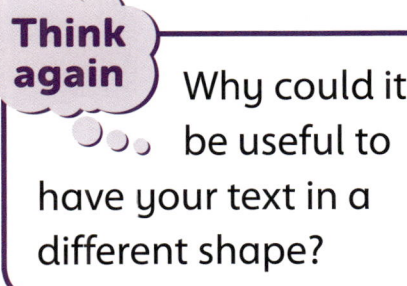 **Extra challenge**

Can you work out how to change the colour or size of the text inside your text box?

In this lesson

You will learn:

➔ how to put text and images together on a page.

Page elements

Leaflets, posters, and brochures all give us information.

We can understand the information better when text and images are used together on a page.

This poster about Lin's favourite hobby has different parts, or elements.

This is the title. The title should be big and easy to read. The title should say what the page is about.

This is the body text. The body text gives interesting information.

My hobby

My name is Lin. I am 7 years old. My hobby is watching birds.

I use binoculars to look up into trees.

The shape gives important information.

The images are about the page topic.

There are more than 10,000 species of birds in the world.

The bee hummingbird is the smallest bird in the world. It is 5 cm long. Hummingbirds can fly backwards.

The caption explains what the image is about.

 **Activity**

Open your 'My hobby' file.

Can you make any improvements to your poster?
You can:

- add new text and images
- change the size of text boxes
- change the size of images
- move text and images around.

 **Extra challenge**

Make a poster about your favourite school subject.

Use text boxes.

Use images.

Save your file.

 **Be creative**

How can you make your title look interesting? Can you change the size, font or colour of the words?

Think again

Look at these posters about hobbies.

Talk to a friend about which poster you like best. Why do you like that poster best?

Check what you know

You have learned

→ how to make a document with words

→ how to make a document with pictures

→ how to save work as a file

→ how to open a saved file.

Test

1 What can you make if you click this icon?

2 Say something else you can add to a poster.

3 How can you find images in a word-processing app?

4 Write down two ways you can make words stand out on a page.

 **Activity**

Open a new file.

Make a poster about someone or something that is important to you. Add:

- a title

- a picture, or image

- a caption

- a text box in a shape that is not a rectangle.

If you have time, add a border to your image.

Save your file.

Self-evaluation

- I answered test questions 1 and 2.

- I started the activity. I made a poster with words in it.

- I answered test questions 1–3.

- I continued the activity. I made a poster with words and images.

- I answered all the test questions.

- I completed the activity. I made the poster look good by using the skills I have learned.

Re-read any parts of the unit you feel unsure about. Try the test and activities again – can you do more this time?

6 Numbers and data: Count wildlife

You will learn

→ how to enter labels and values into a spreadsheet

→ how to use formulas to work out the answer to sums.

A spreadsheet is a computer tool. A spreadsheet will work out the answers to sums.

In this unit you will pretend to be a wildlife ranger at a nature reserve. You will make a spreadsheet and use it to work out sums.

Rangers look after wild animals in nature reserves. Rangers keep animals safe. Rangers need to know what kind of animals there are in the reserve. Rangers need to know how many animals there are in the reserve.

Talk about...

If you were a wildlife ranger, what kinds of animals would you have in your reserve?

Learning outcomes: Enter numbers into a computer and find the answer to a sum

Class activity

Tell your teacher what kinds of animals you would have in your reserve. Count how many of your classmates would like different types of animal.

cell   formula   label
value   addition
subtraction

Did you know?

The Kavango-Zambezi Transfrontier Conservation Area contains 36 national parks, reserves and wildlife areas. It borders the countries of Angola, Botswana, Namibia, Zambia and Zimbabwe.

In this lesson

You will learn:

→ how to put labels into spreadsheet cells.

Spiral back

Last year you learned how to put labels into a spreadsheet. In this lesson you will use those skills again.

Spreadsheet cells

A spreadsheet is made of columns and rows. The columns are named with letters. The rows are numbered. Where a column crosses a row, it is called a **cell**. Every cell is named with its column letter and row number. For example, cell B3.

	A	B
1		
2		
3		
4		

This is cell B3.

Spreadsheet labels

You can put text in spreadsheet cells. A cell with text in it is called a **label**. Labels tell you what the values in the spreadsheet stand for.

To create this spreadsheet:

- Put a title for the spreadsheet in cell A1.

- Enter the names of different animals into other cells in column A.

	A	B	
1	Animals in the reserve		
2			
3	Zebras		
4	Lions		
5	Giraffes		
6	Cheetahs		
7			

Spreadsheet values

You can put numbers in spreadsheet cells. These numbers are called **values**.

● Put values in column B. These numbers say how many animals there are in the reserve.

	A	B
1	Animals in the reserve	
2		
3	Zebras	6
4	Lions	4
5	Giraffes	3
6	Cheetahs	2

 **Activity**

Make a spreadsheet by entering the labels and values shown on this page. Save the file.

 **Extra challenge**

Add an extra animal to the list. How many animals will you have in your reserve? Type the number in the correct cell.

Think again
What is the name of the cell with the label 'giraffes' in it?

In this lesson

You will learn:

➜ how to add up a column of numbers.

Total animals

In this lesson you will find out how many animals there are in the reserve. You will add up all the numbers to find the total.

A spreadsheet will work out the total for you. This is good because:

- it is quicker than working it out yourself
- the computer can add up without making a mistake.

	A	B
1	Animals in the reserve	
2		
3	Zebras	6
4	Lions	4
5	Giraffes	3
6	Cheetahs	2
7		
8	TOTAL	

Type a label

Type a label in the spreadsheet. In this example, the label says 'TOTAL'. It is in cell A8.

Add up

In maths, SUM means the total of something. The formula to add up a total is called AutoSum.

Click the 'Formulas' menu to find the 'AutoSum' button.

Can you find this button?

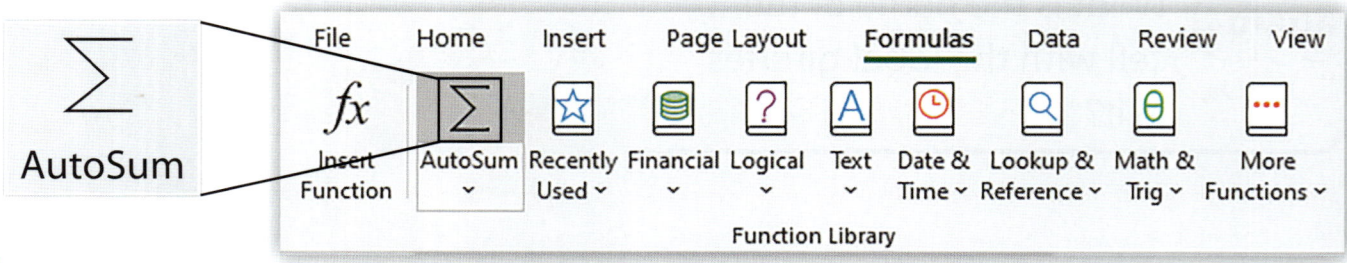

Select the cell

Select the cell where the total will go. In this example, it is cell B8. Now click the 'AutoSum' button.

Press the 'Enter' key. The computer will work out the total.

	A	B	C
1	Animals in the reserve		
2			
3	Zebras	6	
4	Lions	4	
5	Giraffes	3	
6	Cheetahs	2	
7			
8	TOTAL	=SUM(B3:B7)	

	A	B
1	Animals in the reserve	
2		
3	Zebras	6
4	Lions	4
5	Giraffes	3
6	Cheetahs	2
7		
8	TOTAL	15

 **Activity**

Open the file you made in the last lesson. Add a 'Total' label. Use AutoSum to add up the total. Save your work.

 **Extra challenge**

Select the cell with the word 'Total' in it. Make this text red.

 **Think again**

You added up the numbers using AutoSum. Is the result a text label or a number value? How do you know?

In this lesson

You will learn:

➜ what a cell range is

➜ how cell references are used in formulas.

Cell references

You have learned that every spreadsheet cell has a name. The name is the column letter and row number.

The name of a cell is called a cell reference. B3 and B7 are cell references.

Cell ranges

A cell range is a block of cells.

	A	B
1	Animals in the reserve	
2		
3	Zebras	6
4	Lions	4
5	Giraffes	3
6	Cheetahs	2
7		
8	TOTAL	=SUM(B3:B7)

Cells B3 to B7

B3:B7 is a range.

B3:B7 means all the cells from B3 to B7.

What is a formula?

A formula is an instruction to the computer. It tells the computer how to work out a value.

Click on the cell that shows the total number of animals.

The SUM formula

Look at the formula. The formula says:

=SUM(B3:B7)

Each part of this formula means a different thing.

B8	▾ ⋮	✕ ✓ ƒx	=SUM(B3:B7)

	A	B	C
1	Animals in the reserve		
2			
3	Zebras	6	
4	Lions	4	
5	Giraffes	3	
6	Cheetahs	2	
7			
8	TOTAL	15	

The formula   The result

What you see	What it means
=	The equals sign tells the computer that this is a formula.
SUM	Sum means 'add up'.
B3:B7	This is the cell range from B3 to B7.

The formula means 'add up all the numbers in the cell range from B3 to B7'.

Activity

Here are some cell references for the spreadsheet above. Write them on a piece of paper. Next to each one, write the label or value that is in that cell.

- A1
- A3
- B6

Extra challenge

Find the cells that have the names of animals in them. What is the cell range?

Think again

Here is a formula from a different spreadsheet. What does this formula mean? Say in your own words.

=SUM(C2:C5)

6.4 New labels and values

In this lesson

You will learn:

→ how to add new labels and values.

Add a new label

Three animals left the nature reserve. They went to a new home. You will change the spreadsheet to show this new fact.

Click on cell A10. Type the label 'Gone to a new home'.

The label is too big. It spills over into the next cell.

Add a new value

Now add the number. Click on cell B10. Type the value '3'.

	A	B
1	Animals in the reserve	
2		
3	Zebras	6
4	Lions	4
5	Giraffes	3
6	Cheetahs	2
7		
8	TOTAL	15
9		
10	Gone to a new home	

	A	B
1	Animals in the reserve	
2		
3	Zebras	6
4	Lions	4
5	Giraffes	3
6	Cheetahs	2
7		
8	TOTAL	15
9		
10	Gone to a	3

The label is cut off. You cannot see all the words.

Make the column wider

You will make column A wider. This will make enough space for the label.

Move the mouse pointer to the column letters.

Hold down the mouse button and drag. The column will get wider. Now the label is not cut off. The spreadsheet looks better.

> Move the pointer to the line between column A and column B.

	A	B

> When the pointer is in the right place you will see this symbol.

	A	B
1	Animals in the reserve	
2		
3	Zebras	6
4	Lions	4
5	Giraffes	3
6	Cheetahs	2
7		
8	TOTAL	15
9		
10	Go to a new home	3

Activity

Open the file you made in Lesson 6.2. Add the new label and value to show that three animals have gone to a new home.

Extra challenge

Make column A wider so that you can see all the letters in the new label.

Think again You added a new label. It is important that we can read the label. Why is it important?

In this lesson

You will learn:

➔   to make a new spreadsheet formula.

Making formulas

In this lesson you will make a new formula. Your formula will work out how many animals are left in the reserve.

To work out how many animals are left in the reserve, you must find:

The total

MINUS

The number that have gone

Add a label

First add a label. It should say 'Animals left'.

	A	B
1	Animals in the reserve	
2		
3	Zebras	6
4	Lions	4
5	Giraffes	3
6	Cheetahs	2
7		
8	TOTAL	15
9		
10	Gone to a new home	3
11	Animals left	

Start the formula

You will add the formula in the next cell. Select the cell and type the equals sign.

	A	B
1	Animals in the reserve	
2		
3	Zebras	6
4	Lions	4
5	Giraffes	3
6	Cheetahs	2
7		
8	TOTAL	15
9		
10	Gone to a new home	3
11	Animals left	=

Now you must click on the values you want to use. Do it like this:

1 Click on the TOTAL value.

2 Type the minus sign.

3 Click on the number of animals that have gone.

When you press 'Enter' the computer will work out the correct answer.

	A	B
1	Animals in the reserve	
2		
3	Zebras	6
4	Lions	4
5	Giraffes	3
6	Cheetahs	2
7		
8	TOTAL	15
9		
10	Gone to a new home	3
11	Animals left	=B8-B10

 **Activity**

Open the file you made in the last lesson. Enter the label and a formula to show how many animals are left in the nature reserve.

 **Extra challenge**

Change the number of zebras in the reserve by typing a new number. What happens to the total? You will learn more about this in the next lesson.

Think again In this lesson you made a new formula. Write out the formula you made.

 **Be creative**

Make an advert for the nature reserve. Draw the animals. Say how many there are. For example, "We have got 3 giraffes!"

6.6 Changing values

In this lesson

You will learn:

➔ how changing values in a spreadsheet changes the answer.

Cell references

Formulas contain cell references. A cell reference is the name of a cell. When the computer sees a cell reference, it uses the number stored in the cell.

What happens if the number changes? In this lesson you will find out what happens.

Change the values

Column A of your spreadsheet has the names of animals. Column B has the number of animals.

Type new numbers in these cells.

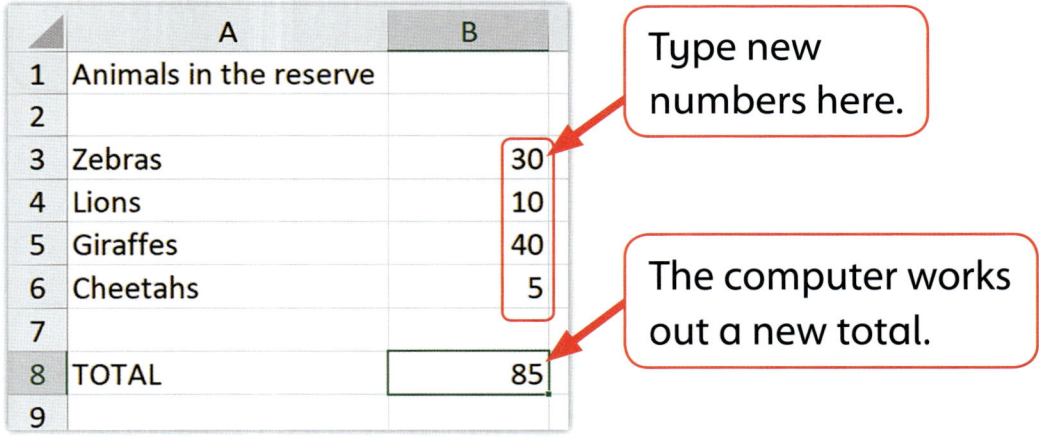

You do not have to type a new total. The computer works it out for you.

Change the number leaving

Find the cell that shows the number of animals that have gone to a new home. Type a new number in the cell.

The computer works out how many animals are left.

	A	B
1	Animals in the reserve	
2		
3	Zebras	30
4	Lions	10
5	Giraffes	40
6	Cheetahs	5
7		
8	TOTAL	85
9		
10	Gone to a new home	20
11	Animals left	65

 **Activity**

Open the file you made in the last lesson. Type new numbers of animals into the spreadsheet. See how the total changes. Add up the numbers yourself on paper, and check that the computer has got it right!

 **Extra challenge**

Your nature reserve can have 100 animals. How many animals will there be of each type? Perhaps you will have 10 lions and 50 zebras? Type different numbers into the cells. Make sure the number of animals left in the reserve does not get bigger than 100.

 **Explore more**

Talk to family and friends about what animals they like to see in a nature reserve. Make a plan for a nature reserve. Choose the type of animals carefully so that people will enjoy their visit. Choose the number of animals carefully so the reserve is not too crowded. If you have time, make a spreadsheet to show your plan.

Check what you know

You have learned

→ how to enter labels and values into a spreadsheet

→ how to use formulas to work out the answer to sums.

Test

Jai has a fruit basket. She made a spreadsheet to show what fruit is in the basket. She entered labels and values. Here is the spreadsheet she made.

	A	B
1	**My fruit basket**	
2		
3	Apples	5
4	Oranges	2
5	Bananas	3
6	Apricots	
7		
8	TOTAL	
9		

1 How many oranges are there?

2 There is one apricot in the basket. Say the name of the cell where this number goes.

3 Jai entered a formula in cell B8 to work out the total amount of fruit. What answer will she see?

Activities

1 Make the spreadsheet that Jai made.

2 Enter the number of apricots in the correct place.

3 Add a formula to work out the total amount of fruit.

4 Change the number of apples to 16. What is the final result in cell B8?

Self-evaluation

●   I answered test question 1.

●   I completed activity 1. I entered labels and values into the spreadsheet.

●   I answered test questions 1 and 2.

●   I completed activities 1–3. I entered the number of apricots in the correct place in the spreadsheet and added an AutoSum formula to the spreadsheet.

●   I answered all the test questions.

●   I completed all the activities. I entered the right formula and found the effect of making changes.

Re-read any parts of the unit you feel unsure about. Try the test and activities again – can you do more this time?

⏻ Digital citizen of the future

Computers can be used to help look after nature and save animals from extinction. Computers can help solve any problem that uses numbers. We can use the power of computers to help look after the environment and the creatures that live in it.

Glossary

add, adding, addition combining two or more numbers to find a total, or how many altogether

algorithm a plan. An algorithm sets out all the actions. It puts them in the right order

border the outside edge of a picture

browser a program that helps you look at pages on websites

cell a square on the spreadsheet grid

cell reference the name of a cell in the spreadsheet grid, formed by combining the column letter and the row number

command an instruction that tells the computer what to do. When you run a program, the computer follows the commands. In Scratch, each block is a command

depends on sometimes an action depends on another. It uses the results of the other action. The action that 'depends on' must come later

device something people make to do a useful task

document a file that can hold text and sometimes images. It can be stored electronically or printed out on paper

download copying a file from one computer to your computer, for example using an internet connection

event something that happens that affects a program – for example, the event that starts a program

event block a block that starts a program script

file a collection of information stored on a computer. Each file has its own name

forever loop a control structure. Commands inside the loop will repeat 'forever' (while the program is running)

formula instructions for the spreadsheet to calculate a value. In a spreadsheet, formulas begin with an equals sign =

hardware the parts that make up a computer

images pictures

independent sometimes two actions are independent. That means they do not need each other. It does not matter which action comes first and which comes second

input devices that let you put information or data into a computer

internet a network of computers that goes across the whole world

keyboard a device that lets you type letters and other characters into a computer

label text entered into a spreadsheet cell

laptop a small computer that can be moved around

load a program get a program from storage. Now you can run the program

memory part of a computer. The memory of a computer stores information using on and off signals

monitor the screen of a computer. It is an output device

mouse a device you can use to move the cursor around the screen. Some computers have a trackpad instead of a mouse

necessary what is needed. A plan has all the actions that are necessary

network a way of linking computers so they can send signals to each other

output information that comes out of a computer. An output device lets the computer make output, for example, the computer screen or a printer

personal information things about you that tells others who you are and where they can find you, such as your address

printer a device that sends output from the computer onto paper

private information secret things about you, such as a password

processor this is at the centre of a computer system – it controls all the other parts of the computer system. If you tell the computer to do a task, the processor is the part that makes sure it happens

programmer a person who writes a program

random location if something is random you do not know what it will be. If the sprite jumps to a random location, you do not know where the sprite will jump to

run a program a series of commands. When you run a program, the computer follows the commands

safe protected from danger

save to keep and store something for future use

screen part of a computer system that shows the output from the computer. A screen on a desktop computer is called a 'monitor'

search engine a program that collects information about websites so that you can find them easily

sequence the order of actions. A plan must show actions in the right sequence

speaker hardware that connects to a computer to make sound

sprite an image on the computer screen. It is controlled by the program

subtract, subtraction taking one number away from another

text box a rectangular frame into which you can type words

touchscreen a device used for input and output. A touchscreen shows you output on the screen. Touch the screen to make input

upload copy a file from your computer to a another computer, for example a web page

user the person who uses a computer or a program

value a number in a spreadsheet. A value can be used in calculations

website a set of web pages, connected to the world wide web

wireless signals that go between devices without using wires